How to Bitcoin

Kristian Kho, Khor Win Win, Crystaline Loo,
Lee Shu Wei, Shaun Paul Lee, Teh Sze Jin,
Bobby Ong

CONTENTS

INTRODUCTION

Welcome to CoinGecko's second book, **How to Bitcoin**! We received so much positive feedback on our first book, *How to DeFi*, that we decided to write this one!

Bitcoin was the first cryptocurrency that got us started on our journey. Our understanding of Bitcoin has opened up many opportunities for us, and in these pages, we hope to share our collective knowledge with you. In How to Bitcoin, you will learn of Bitcoin's transformative aspects and how it can open new opportunities for you too.

Bitcoin is not new. As we write this, it is 12 years old. That being said, it is still early and not too late to learn about Bitcoin and its implications for the future. Perhaps you would have heard of Bitcoin as this "magic Internet money" with revolutionary potential. We hope to debunk that and put together what makes Bitcoin revolutionary other than just "magic."

How to Bitcoin is written for beginners with simple analogies to help you understand how it works. There are step-by-step guides to show you how to buy and secure your first bitcoin. It will be a relatively light read if you already have a deep understanding of Bitcoin. If so, we would be honored to receive your suggestions on improving this book.

Lastly, we see a future where owning a bitcoin is a matter of choice and foresight rather than ignorance. We hope this book can contribute to making that a reality.

CoinGecko Research Team
Kristian Kho, Khor Win Win, Crystaline Loo, Lee Shu Wei, Shaun Paul Lee, Teh Sze Jin, Bobby Ong
1 January 2021

PART 1: WHAT IS BITCOIN?

CHAPTER 1: BITCOIN AND MONEY

Bitcoin is a peer-to-peer electronic payment system that allows parties to transact with each other without the need to use any trusted third-party intermediaries. It is an alternative to our traditional financial system, where payments need to be routed through financial institutions.

When you use Bitcoin, you do not need to trust a centralised entity such as a government, a bank, or a financial institution. For example, in the traditional financial system, using PayPal requires that you trust PayPal's ability to make transactions. Paying with your Mastercard requires that you trust Mastercard, your bank, your merchant's bank, and other payment processors to clear your transaction.

Even using cash requires you and your counterparty to trust your government officials. As recently as 2016 the Prime Minister of India demonetized the 500 and 1,000 rupee notes causing significant immediate volatility.[1]

Bitcoin is a payment protocol and a cryptocurrency itself. This protocol is a payment network that allows for transactions to be routed without relying on any third parties. It is powered by a new technology known as the

---

[1] (2016, November 8). Rupee notes in India: Narendra Modi just banned Rs500 and ....
Retrieved November 26, 2020, from https://qz.com/india/830774/rupee-notes-in-india-narendra-modi-just-banned-rs500-and-rs1000-notes-to-fight-corruption-and-terrorism/

blockchain. Bitcoin is also known as a cryptocurrency, a type of virtual currency, because transactions are secured using cryptography.

For the purposes of this book, we will be representing 'Bitcoin' with a capitalized 'B' whenever we refer to the Bitcoin protocol and 'bitcoin' with a lowercase 'b' when we refer to the bitcoin cryptocurrency.

Bitcoin distinguishes itself from traditional fiat currencies as it is not backed by any government, central bank, or centralized authority. Instead, it is created, stored, and distributed digitally on a public, decentralized ledger that follows a strict set of simple rules.

This is the philosophy that created Bitcoin—the ability to operate a financial system in a decentralized manner without the need to trust any centralized intermediary.

Government Money

Before we continue with bitcoin itself, it may be worth revisiting the money that we use on a day-to-day basis.

For something that almost everyone on Earth labors for and cherishes after, few understand how money functions and even less comprehend the intricacies of the fiat monetary system.

> *"It is well enough that people of the nation do not understand our banking and monetary system, for if they did, I believe there would be a revolution before tomorrow morning."*
>
> —Quote attributed to Henry Ford

"Government Money" is what is known as *fiat currency*, or in simple English, "Money by Decree".

Fiat is derived from the Latin word "fiat", which essentially means "let it be done". Fiat has been deemed as money because it is mandated by governments as being legal tender by law and thus must be accepted as a valid form of payment under the scrutiny of our legal jurisdiction.

With most things in government, money is handled with a top-down approach. National leaders decide every facet of the monetary system and regular folks follow the rules that have been set.

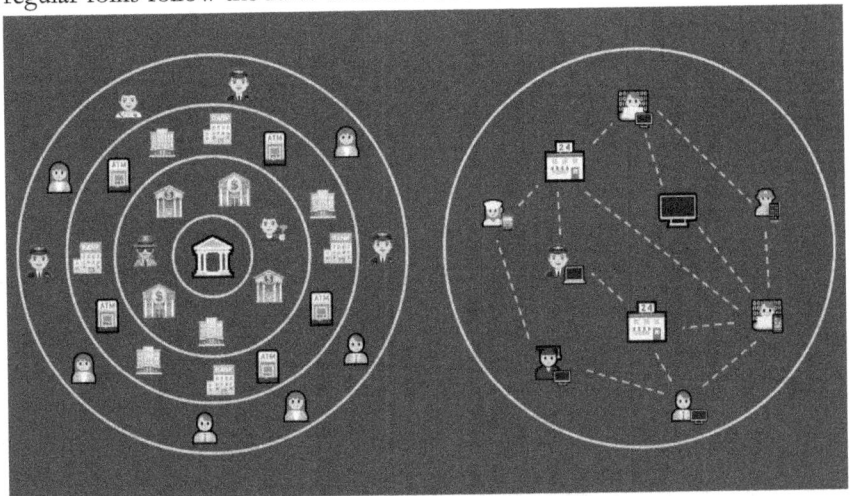

Fiat's layered bureaucratic system vs. Bitcoin's peer-to-peer system.

In an ideal world, a top-down fiat monetary system isn't all that bad. After all, not everyone is an expert in economics and finance; it is perfectly acceptable to just use a robust value-transfer system without needing to worry about anything as one goes on with their daily lives.

However, for the past century or so, this has not been the case.

Without going into too much detail, the rules governing paper money, more specifically the US Dollar, changed in 1913.[2] Paper money that used to be "backed by gold" became paper money "backed by the government". During this period, the Federal Reserve (Fed) at least tried to tie the value of the dollar with gold. Things took a turn for the worse in 1971 when the Fed stopped trying and decided that the Dollar was worth whatever it says it was worth.[3]

---

2 (2020, July 27). 1913 Federal Reserve Act Definition – Investopedia. Retrieved November 10, 2020, from https://www.investopedia.com/terms/f/1913-federal-reserve-act.asp

3 (2013, March 13). President Nixon: The Man Who Sold the World Fiat Money .... Retrieved November 10, 2020, from https://blogs.cfainstitute.org/investor/2013/03/13/president-nixon-the-man-who-sold-the-world-fiat-money/

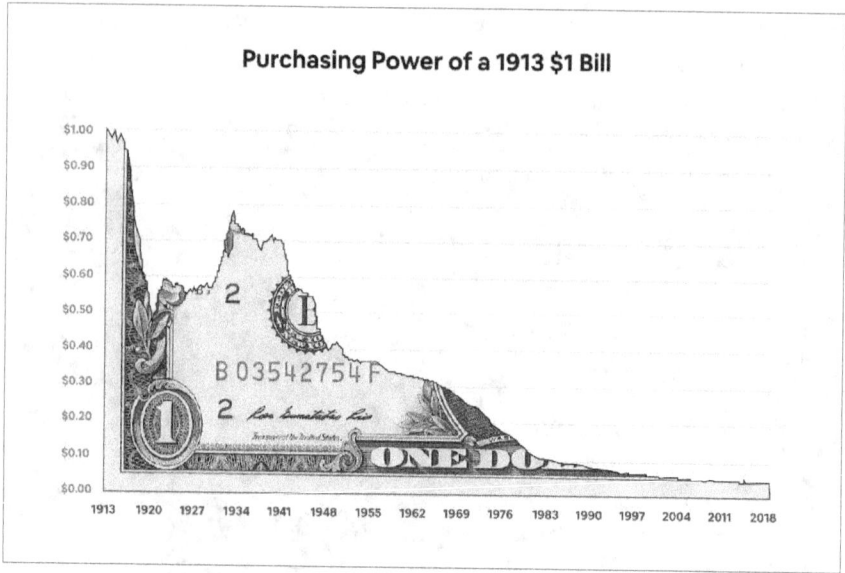

Data from St. Louis Federal Reserve

2008 Financial Crisis

The above sets the scene for what was about to happen when the whole world economy crashed down during the 2008 Financial Crisis.

The 2008 Financial Crisis in the United States was one of the worst economic disasters in history, crumbling the world's financial and banking system.[4] Many large financial institutions and banks tragically fell apart. Amongst the fallen were Lehman Brothers and Bear Stearns.

This crisis stemmed from subprime mortgage loans, which in simple terms were loans issued to high-risk borrowers who do not qualify for conventional loans.[5] These loans were then repackaged multiple times into complex derivatives. Bad loans combined with widespread fraudulent practices across various financial institutions exacerbated the housing

---

[4] (2019, August 1). A History Guide to the 2008 Financial Crisis: What Caused the .... Retrieved November 12, 2020, from https://www.historyextra.com/period/modern/financial-crisis-crash-explained-facts-causes/

[5] (2008, April 27). Moody's - Credit Rating - Mortgages - The New York Times. Retrieved November 12, 2020, from https://www.nytimes.com/2008/04/27/magazine/27Credit-t.html

bubble. It created a ticking time bomb that ultimately blew up into the 2008 Financial Crisis.

The main reason which caused the credit crisis was the naïve assumption that interest rates will continuously stay low and residential home prices will continually increase in price. When both these assumptions broke, many of the subprime borrowers could not repay their home loans and had their homes repossessed by the banks.

This caused a devastating ripple effect to the economy. To salvage the economy, the U.S Treasury bailed out 'too big to fail' banks.[6]

The 2008 financial crisis highlighted the fragility of our traditional financial and banking system. Banks were supposed to be the central trustworthy authorities safeguarding the money we deposit and governing our monetary system's health. However, they have failed miserably to do so.

The Birth of a Financial Alternative

It is against this backdrop of the global monetary crisis that the Bitcoin whitepaper was published pseudonymously by an entity known as "Satoshi Nakamoto". Satoshi released the Bitcoin whitepaper on a cryptography-focused mailing list on 31st October 2008.[7] The 9-page whitepaper outlines a new financial system with a new cryptocurrency called bitcoin.

The sudden appearance of Bitcoin's whitepaper during this period is almost too good of a coincidence. Compounded by the growing distrust of the fiat financial system at that time, Bitcoin grew in popularity from an obscure online forum into a viable financial alternative now.

On 3rd January 2009, The Genesis Block started the Bitcoin Network, bringing the world's first decentralized payment system to life.[8] The

---

[6] Too Big to Fail: a theory that asserts certain companies and institutions are too large and interconnected to the fabric of the economy that it must not fail.

[7] (n.d.). Bitcoin P2P e-cash paper – Cryptography mailing list. Retrieved November 10, 2020, from https://www.metzdowd.com/pipermail/cryptography/2008-October/014810.html

[8] (n.d.). Bitcoin / Blocks — Blockchair. Retrieved November 12, 2020, from https://blockchair.com/bitcoin/blocks

resulting alternative payment network allows for the transfer of value over the Internet electronically in a peer-to-peer manner, without the need for a centralized authority overseeing the transaction.

```
00000000  01 00 00 00 00 00 00 00  00 00 00 00 00 00 00 00   ................
00000010  00 00 00 00 00 00 00 00  00 00 00 00 00 00 00 00   ................
00000020  00 00 00 00 3B A3 ED FD  7A 7B 12 B2 7A C7 2C 3E   ....;£íý z{.²zÇ,>
00000030  67 76 8F 61 7F C8 1B C3  88 8A 51 32 3A 9F B8 AA   gv.a.È.Ã.ŠQ2:Ÿ.ª
00000040  4B 1E 5E 4A 29 AB 5F 49  FF FF 00 1D 1D AC 2B 7C   K.^J)«_Iÿÿ..¬+|
00000050  01 01 00 00 00 01 00 00  00 00 00 00 00 00 00 00   ................
00000060  00 00 00 00 00 00 00 00  00 00 00 00 00 00 00 00   ................
00000070  00 00 00 00 00 00 FF FF  FF FF 4D 04 FF FF 00 1D   ......ÿÿÿÿM.ÿÿ..
00000080  01 04 45 54 68 65 20 54  69 6D 65 73 20 30 33 2F   ..EThe Times 03/
00000090  4A 61 6E 2F 32 30 30 39  20 43 68 61 6E 63 65 6C   Jan/2009 Chancel
000000A0  6C 6F 72 20 6F 6E 20 62  72 69 6E 6B 20 6F 66 20   lor on brink of 
000000B0  73 65 63 6F 6E 64 20 62  61 69 6C 6F 75 74 20 66   second bailout f
000000C0  6F 72 20 62 61 6E 6B 73  FF FF FF FF 01 00 F2 05   or banksÿÿÿÿ..ò.
000000D0  2A 01 00 00 00 43 41 04  67 8A FD B0 FE 55 48 27   *....CA.gŠý°þUH'
000000E0  19 67 F1 A6 71 30 B7 10  5C D6 A8 28 E0 39 09 A6   .gñ¦q0·.\Ö¨(à9.¦
000000F0  79 62 E0 EA 1F 61 DE B6  49 F6 BC 3F 4C EF 38 C4   ybàê.aÞ¶Iö¼?Lï8Ä
00000100  F3 55 04 E5 1E C1 12 DE  5C 38 4D F7 BA 0B 8D 57   óU.å.Á.Þ\8M÷º..W
00000110  8A 4C 70 2B 6B F1 1D 5F  AC 00 00 00 00            ŠLp+kñ._¬....
```

Being the first block on the Bitcoin blockchain, the Genesis Block is unique as it does not contain a previous block reference compared to the subsequent blocks mined. It may seem that Satoshi was fully aware of the financial failures of the time and understood the invention of Bitcoin is an apparent challenge to the financial and monetary institutions. Within the Genesis Block, Satoshi left a string of characters that may have served as the call to Bitcoin's purpose as well as a timestamp to prove that Bitcoin started on the day itself.

The words *"The Times 03/Jan/2009 Chancellor on brink of second bailout for banks"* were etched on the Bitcoin blockchain to be seen by all for eternity. This Easter egg is a direct copy of The Times headline of the same date.

THE TIMES

Max 5C, min -5C | Saturday January 3 2009 timesonline.co.uk No 69523 | £1.50

Eat Out from £5
More than 900 great restaurants, including
four **Gordon Ramsay** favourites from £15

Start collecting tokens today Pullout Inside

Israel prepares to send tanks and troops into Gaza

Israel allowed foreigners to flee the Gaza Strip as it prepared for a ground offensive. At least 430 Palestinians were killed in a week of airstrikes News, page 3

Michael Sheen
Frost, Nixon
and me
Magazine

Working mums
So that's how
she does it
Body&Soul

Detox in style
The best spas
on the planet
Travel

Chancellor on brink of second bailout for banks

Billions may be needed as lending squeeze tightens

Salmon Rushdie
I Won't Marry
Again
Pages 22, 23

Francis Elliott Deputy Political Editor
Gary Duncan Economics Editor

Alistair Darling has been forced to consider a second bailout for banks as the lending drought worsens.

The Chancellor will decide within weeks whether to pump billions more into the economy as evidence mounts that the £37billion part-nationalisation last year has failed to keep credit flowing. Options include cash injections, offering banks cheaper state guarantees to raise money privately or buying up "toxic assets", The Times has learnt.

The Bank of England revealed yester-

day that, despite intense pressure, the banks curbed lending in the final quarter of last year and plan even tighter restrictions in the coming months. Its findings will alarm the Treasury.

The Bank is expected to take yet more aggressive action this week by cutting the base rate from its current level of 2 per cent. Doing so would reduce the cost of borrowing, but have little effect on the availability of loans.

Whitehall sources said that ministers planned to "keep the banks on the boil" but accepted that they need more help to restore lending levels.

Formally, the Treasury plans to focus

on state-backed gurantees to encourage private finance, but a number of interventions are on the table, including further injections of taxpayers' cash. Under one option, a "bad bank" would be created to dispose of bad

debts. The Treasury would take bad loans off the hands of troubled banks, perhaps swapping them for government bonds. The toxic assets, blamed for poisoning the financial system, would be parked in a state vehicle or "bad bank" that would manage them and attempt to dispose of them while "detoxifying" the mainstream banking system.

The idea would mirror the initial proposal by Henry Paulson, the US Treasury Secretary, to underpin the American banking system by buying

Continued on page 6, col 1
Leading article, page 2

99p
Pub chain cuts the
price of a pint from
£1.69 to 1989 levels
Business, page 47

Giant Killing?
Guide to the FA
Cup Third Round
Sport

Digitized copy of The Times article, "Chancellor on brink of second bailout for banks" from January 3, 2009

11

Fun Fact

The first 50 BTC block reward in the Genesis Block is unspendable. Till this day, it remains a mystery if Satoshi Nakamoto deliberately coded it to be non-transferable or if it was a mistake.

The Genesis Block's reward recipient address 1A1zP1eP5QGefi2DMPTfTL5SLmv7DivfNa, suspected to be owned by Satoshi, has been receiving donations from fans.[9] At the time of writing, it has accumulated a total of 68.3 BTC.

Characteristics of Bitcoin

These are some of the core characteristics of Bitcoin which makes it unique:
1. Clearly-defined monetary policy
2. Permissionless, peer-to-peer system
3. Open-source, transparent, and decentralized ledger
4. Highly fungible, durable, portable, and divisible
5. Digital money

1. **Clearly Defined Monetary Policy**

   A crucial characteristic of bitcoin is that it is a decentralized currency, unlike fiat currency which is controlled by a centralized authority such as a central bank.[10]

   Central banks have the ability to issue new money at their will. According to the European Central Bank, "Central banks are protected from insolvency due to their ability to create money and can therefore operate with negative equity."[11]

   Recall the 2008 Financial Crisis that was mentioned earlier. With the aid of the Fed, Quantitative Easing (QE) was used to salvage the crisis.

---

[9] (n.d.). Address: 1A1zP1eP5QGefi2DMPTfTL5SLmv7DivfNa .... Retrieved November 12, 2020, from
https://www.blockchain.com/btc/address/1A1zP1eP5QGefi2DMPTfTL5SLmv7DivfNa

[10] (n.d.). What is Bitcoin? Price in USD, Mining, Bitcoin ... – Bitcoin Wiki. Retrieved November 10, 2020, from https://en.bitcoinwiki.org/wiki/Bitcoin

[11] (n.d.). Profit distribution and loss coverage rules for central banks. Retrieved November 10, 2020, from https://www.ecb.europa.eu/pub/pdf/scpops/ecbop169.en.pdf

This highlights the immense control that central banks have with regards to monetary policy.

A key feature of Bitcoin is its scarcity—there will only ever be 21 million bitcoins in circulation. This cap is final and cannot be altered. Bitcoin differentiates itself from traditional fiat currency with its limitless supply.

Bitcoin is also similar to gold in the sense that it has to be mined into circulation. However, unlike gold, which needs to be mined physically in actual ores, bitcoin is mined digitally.[12] This is why bitcoin has often been referred to as "digital gold".

For every block created, new bitcoins will be mined as block rewards to Bitcoin miners. This will be explained in detail in the coming chapters. At the time of writing, 18.5 million bitcoins, or more than two-thirds of all bitcoins have already been mined.

2. **Permissionless, Peer-to-Peer System**
   Let's say Alice wants to send $1,000 to Bob. Traditionally, the pathway taken to do so would look something like this:

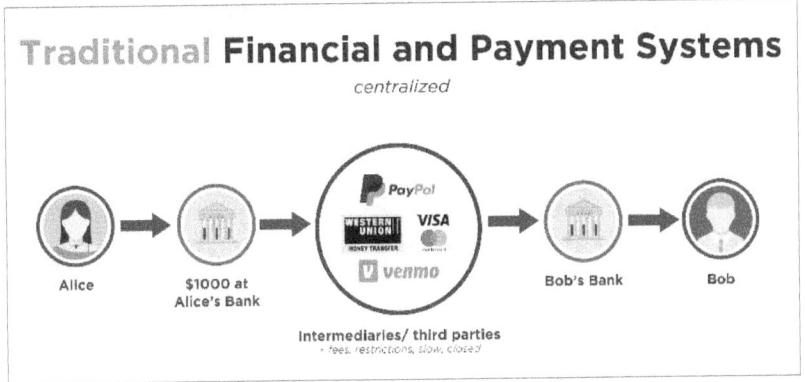

---

[12] Bitcoin Mining, or in technical terms "Proof of Work", is the backbone in which the Bitcoin network and economics operates. We will uncover more about Bitcoin mining in a later chapter.

Alice would have to not only rely on Alice's and Bob's banks, but also a slew of intermediaries and third party financial institutions and service providers depending on the requirements of Alice's and Bob's banks.

This system of sending money presents inefficiencies and bureaucracy. Each of the companies may charge a fee, making the transaction expensive. There are also various money transfer laws that need to be followed.

For example, if Alice is a US citizen and Bob is an Iranian, the transaction will never happen due to international sanction laws.[13]

Even if a transaction happens locally, governments can arbitrarily cancel the transaction or even confiscate the money altogether.

In July 2020, Hong Kong passed legislation allowing the government to freeze bank accounts and assets of people who have been deemed to "endanger national security".[14] This threat may be used as a tool to suppress the freedom of speech of the people amidst the ongoing political turmoil.

Using Bitcoin, intermediaries like banks or payment processors are no longer needed to oversee transactions. Let's take a look at the scenario if Alice were to transfer $1,000 worth of bitcoin to Bob:

---

[13] (2020, October 9). Iran sanctions: US moves to isolate 'major' banks – BBC News. Retrieved January 20, 2021, from https://www.bbc.com/news/world-middle-east-54476894

[14] (2020, July 6). Hong Kong security law: Police handed power to do .... Retrieved November 10, 2020, from https://hongkongfp.com/2020/07/06/breaking-hong-kong-security-law-police-handed-power-to-do-warrantless-searches-freeze-assets-intercept-comms-control-internet/

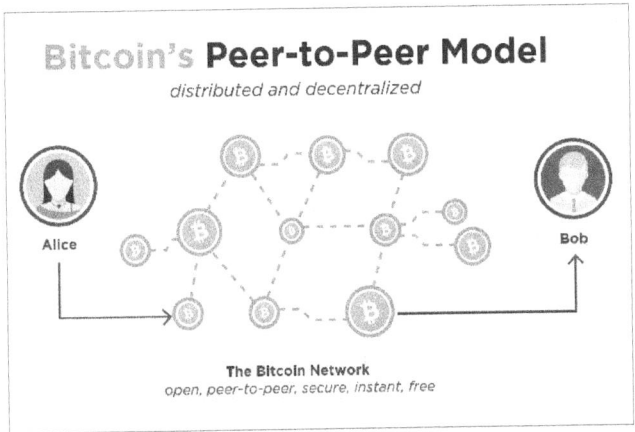

Using the Bitcoin network, Alice directly transfers value over to Bob without any authorization from anyone, hence the term "peer-to-peer". The removal of the middlemen like the bank is profound as this bypasses the many potential issues associated with central authorities and third parties.

By removing third parties from the transfer of value, we remove the ability for these middlemen to exert authority over our financial transactions. PayPal is famous for freezing users' accounts for various reasons; you can find many people complaining about this issue online.[15]

Bitcoin allows us to have full control of our own assets without the need to trust any institutions or third parties. With this control, no one can unilaterally freeze or revoke our assets without our permission.

The power now goes back to individuals. Anyone, no matter who or where they are, can now directly engage in the transfer of value and economic activity with another person without any third-party's permission.

---

[15] (2018, August 21). PayPal Account Limitations: what they are and what you can ....
Retrieved November 17, 2020, from
https://www.paypal.com/us/brc/article/understanding-account-limitations

3. **Open-Source, Transparent and Decentralized Ledger**

The Bitcoin protocol, the set of code that powers the Bitcoin network, is released under the MIT License more popularly known as open-source software.[16] [17] This means that the code is open for everyone to see, inspect, copy, and propose improvements. Anyone is free to suggest improvements to Bitcoin, thereby aligning incentives amongst the Bitcoin community.[18]

The Bitcoin ledger is distributed globally. It is decentralized and no single entity is able to tamper or manipulate the data contained in the blockchain. Anyone who tries to unilaterally manipulate the data on their ledger will be known immediately because their ledger will not be similar to the ledger maintained by everyone else.

This means that no one fully owns or controls Bitcoin. No entity—not even governments—can annihilate Bitcoin's existence.

To give a simple analogy to explain this concept of a decentralized ledger, let's take a look at a game of Monopoly played between 4 friends. Instead of distributing Monopoly paper money to all 4 players during the game, a blank notebook and a pen is given to each player. Each player will record the amount of money that all 4 players have at each turn during the game.

After every turn, everyone pauses to check each other's notebooks to ensure that it tallies with everyone else's records. This way, any player who tries to cheat will have the discrepancy caught immediately and can be easily disqualified from the game.

4. Highly Fungible, Durable, Portable, and Divisible

Bitcoin is also a type of money that is highly fungible, durable, portable and divisible.

---

[16] (n.d.). bitcoin/COPYING at master bitcoin/bitcoin GitHub. Retrieved November 10, 2020, from https://github.com/bitcoin/bitcoin/blob/master/COPYING

[17] (n.d.). What is open source software? | Opensource.com. Retrieved November 10, 2020, from https://opensource.com/resources/what-open-source

[18] (2018, December 15). Who Controls Bitcoin Core? – Cypherpunk Cogitations. Retrieved November 24, 2020, from https://blog.lopp.net/who-controls-bitcoin-core-/

Fungibility is a concept where things are mutually interchangeable. Bitcoin is fungible because each bitcoin can be easily replaceable with another bitcoin.

Bitcoin is also highly durable because it cannot be easily destroyed by natural elements unlike paper money. So long as the private keys to your bitcoin are stored safely and are not lost, you will have access to your bitcoin.

Because bitcoin is a form of digital money, it is incredibly portable. You can bring your entire net wealth with you wherever you go with just the private keys. This is significant especially to people who live in countries without a stable government. With bitcoin, these people can pack their bags and move to a stable country while still retaining their wealth.

Bitcoin is also divisible to 8 decimal places. The smallest unit for bitcoin is 0.00000001 BTC, also known as a satoshi. This was named as a tribute to the creator of Bitcoin, Satoshi Nakamoto. This means that you do not need to send or own 1 whole bitcoin but can send small fractions of bitcoin to pay for goods and services.

5. **Digital Money**
    Being a digital currency is important because it means that the money we use can be easily programmed to do highly customizable things.

    Antony Lewis mentioned in his writing that money in your bank accounts are not really programmable because the money in each bank is technically different. Dollars in Citibank and JP Morgan have different legal agreements and have different logic and constraints.[19]
    Because there is no ledger referencing the money stored in different bank accounts, this makes it hard for money to be programmed to follow certain rules.

---

[19] (2020, April 26). What Actually is Programmable Money? – LinkedIn. Retrieved November 18, 2020, from https://www.linkedin.com/pulse/what-actually-programmable-money-antony-lewis

With Bitcoin, there is the bitcoin ledger where programmers can set rules to program escrow, notaries, design payouts and dividends.[20] This concept of universal cash will become increasingly important as we move towards machine-to-machine payments in the future.

Bitcoin vs Gold vs Fiat Currencies

Bitcoin has often been compared to gold and fiat currencies like the US Dollar. There are several similarities and differences between these various forms of asset classes. This table here provides a summary of the various characteristics of bitcoin relative to gold and fiat currencies:

Traits of Money	Gold	Fiat Currencies	Bitcoin
Fungible (Interchangeable)	High	High	High
Non-Consumable	High	High	High
Portability	Moderate	High	High
Durable	High	Moderate	High
Highly Divisible	Moderate	Moderate	High
Secure (Cannot be counterfeited)	Moderate	Moderate	High
Easily Transactable	Low	High	High
Scarce	Moderate	Low	High
Sovereign (Government issued)	Low	High	Low
Decentralized	Low	Low	High
Programmable	Low	Low	High

---

[20] (2013, September 10). Inside Bitcoin, The Programmable Currency For Our Digital .... Retrieved November 18, 2020, from https://techcrunch.com/2013/09/10/disrupt-sf-13-bitcoin-panel/

Use Cases of Bitcoin – Can bitcoin be our new money?

With the defining characteristics of bitcoin being so profoundly advantageous over the traditional financial system, the big question remains: Why isn't bitcoin replacing fiat money? Let's take a look at how bitcoin measures up to the 3 classical functions of money:

1. Medium of Exchange
2. Store of Value
3. Unit of Account

Medium of Exchange

As a medium of exchange, bitcoin does fulfill this function of money as payments can be made anytime in a peer-to-peer manner without any third party. No one needs to approve your transaction or even have the ability to stop you from making your transaction.

That being said, bitcoin has not reached wide-scale global adoption and is therefore not treated as a suitable medium of exchange globally. Bitcoin is prevalent within its community of supporters and used interchangeably as a suitable medium of exchange. In fact, many in the Bitcoin community actually prefer being paid in bitcoin.

Despite the lower cost for merchants to accept bitcoin, it is still rarely accepted by merchants on a global level due to the prevalence of credit cards. However, there are several merchants that accept bitcoin using crypto payment processors. This allows you to pay in bitcoin, which then converts into fiat currency for the merchant.

In less stable economies, we see bitcoin being used as an alternative to fiat currencies for payments. This may be due to macroeconomic mismanagement such as high inflation and the depreciation of the fiat currency.

Store of Value

Bitcoin is an extremely volatile asset class. Its price has gone from pennies in its early days to $20,000 during its peak in early-2018. As a store of value, it does a pretty bad job at maintaining price stability in the short-term. Depending on when you purchased bitcoin, it may or may not store value reasonably well in the short-term due to its volatile nature.

However, in the long term, it may potentially be an excellent store of value relative to fiat currencies. Similar to gold, bitcoin is considered an excellent long-term store of value due to its scarcity and finite supply. This scarce nature resulted in bitcoin often being referred to as "digital gold".

While gold has been identified as a safe haven commodity for thousands of years, bitcoin has only until recently been seen as a safe asset.

Our fiat currency is constantly being inflated away each year. Using an inflation calculator with the US Consumer Price Index data, an item that was purchased for $1 in the year 2000 would cost you $1.51 in 2020.[21] This means that the value of the US Dollar has depreciated by 51% in just the last 20 years.

Safe Haven for Troubled Nations

Troubled countries such as Venezuela, Zimbabwe and Argentina are suffering from one of the worst economic crises in modern times. Their political instability and distorted monetary policies caused extreme hyperinflation and have diminished the value of their fiat currencies to practically nothing. For example, inflation in Venezuela was 1,700,000% in 2018.[22]

Bitcoin has become especially relevant in these counties for residents to hedge against their rapid corroding fiat currency. As a result, cryptocurrency adoption has soared in Venezuela, ranking 3rd on Chainalysis's Global Crypto Adoption Index in 2020.[23]

In countries with unstable economics such as Venezuela, Zimbabwe and Argentina, residents have lost their life savings due to hyperinflation as a result of the mismanagement of the country's monetary policy. Many people have no other option to retain their wealth and many have resorted

---

[21] (n.d.). Inflation Calculator. Retrieved January 20, 2021, from https://www.usinflationcalculator.com/

[22] (n.d.). Inflación de 2018 cerró en 1.698.488%, según la Asamblea .... Retrieved November 26, 2020, from https://efectococuyo.com/economia/inflacion-de-2018-cerro-en-1-698-488-segun-la-asamblea-nacional/

[23] (2020, August 27). Cryptocurrency usage in Venezuela – Chainalysis blog. Retrieved November 20, 2020, from https://blog.chainalysis.com/reports/venezuela-cryptocurrency-market-2020

to using bitcoin as a store of value to hedge against their eroding local currency.

Unit of Account

As a unit of account, bitcoin does not perform well due to its volatile nature compared to fiat currencies. With bitcoin's price fluctuating constantly, the real economic value of goods and services becomes hard to be determined, measured, and compared. This makes it extremely difficult to price items in bitcoin.

For example, retailers that accept bitcoin as a method of payment do not price their items at a fixed bitcoin rate. Instead, items are priced in fiat currency terms and are then allowed to constantly fluctuate with the price movement of bitcoin. Therefore, bitcoin functions as an intermediary between the fiat currency and the items being exchanged.[24]

We have not reached a stage where bitcoin's price volatility reduces and people can denominate goods and services in terms of bitcoin. Some people have speculated that volatility will reduce as bitcoin matures but we have not seen this narrative play out yet.

Bitcoin is divisible to the eighth decimal place, down to 0.00000001 BTC, which is equivalent to one satoshi. Research has shown that there is a strong upward trend in the use of bitcoin's highest available degree of precision (one satoshi) over the years, suggesting that the idea of bitcoin being a unit of account remains a pipe dream.[25]

---

[24] (n.d.). Why Bitcoin Is Not a Viable Currency Option – Knowledge .... Retrieved November 24, 2020, from https://kw.wharton.upenn.edu/kwfellows/files/2018/06/2018-08-30-Bitcoin-Student-Series.pdf

[25] (2020, January 27). Growth In The Level Of Precision Of Bitcoin ... – BitMEX Blog. Retrieved November 24, 2020, from https://blog.bitmex.com/bitcoin-transaction-output-value-precision/

> **Fun Fact**
>
> On 22nd May 2010, Laszlo Hanyecz bought 2 Domino's pizzas with 10,000 bitcoins.[26] He is known as the first person to make a commercial transaction using bitcoin. At the time of writing, the 10,000 BTC is worth a whopping $130 million!
>
> Since then, May 22nd has been celebrated in the community each year as the "Bitcoin Pizza Day".

Closing Thoughts

All in all, it is important to realize that Bitcoin's inception was not intended to be a replacement of the fiat currencies that you use to buy your daily dose of caffeine.

Rather, Bitcoin's primary existence serves to provide an alternative financial system that can operate without the need to trust and rely on third-party financial institutions. Bitcoin's inception revolutionizes the way we perform transactions using a decentralized, peer-to-peer payment system.

---

[26] (2010, May 18). Pizza for bitcoins? – Bitcoin Forum. Retrieved January 20, 2021, from https://bitcointalk.org/index.php?topic=137.0

CHAPTER 2: ANATOMY OF BITCOIN

Now that you understand Bitcoin's background, birth and reasonings, let's find out how Bitcoin works.

Bitcoin was set up to be a peer-to-peer digital cash system that does not require an intermediary to settle a transaction. By decentralizing, democratizing and allowing everyone in the world access to a single permissionless payment network, Bitcoin disrupts the traditional financial system in the same way that the Internet has done to information and media.[27]

In order to make this possible, Satoshi designed a distributed ledger system where every participant in the network can inspect and verify every transaction in the network. We will explore how you as an individual can do so as well, after equipping yourself with the knowledge of some of the terms and concepts in the Bitcoin network.

The following chapter uncovers the anatomy of Bitcoin and its underlying blockchain. There will be several technical terms that may not be immediately useful for your day-to-day use. However, as they say, you do not need to understand the carburetor to drive a car, but knowing so might save you down the road.

---

[27] Antonopoulos, Andreas M. (2017). *The Internet of Money*. Merkle Bloom.

The Bitcoin Ledger

One way to envision the workings of the Bitcoin blockchain is to expand upon the Monopoly analogy that we briefly mentioned in the previous chapter. We imagined a game of Monopoly played between four friends. Let's call the players in this game Alice, Bob, Charlie, and Debbie.

Instead of distributing the usual Monopoly paper money to all four players, a blank notebook and pen is given to each player instead. Each player will record transactions made by all players during the game.

For simplicity, we will assume the following for the Monopoly game:
1. Players start at different parts of the board and have 10 BTC each.
2. They will also be given a random selection of Monopoly properties which they will pay rent to each other.
3. With each turn, transactions are recorded on a new page in the notebook and only one player can pass "Go" in each round to collect the 50 BTC reward.

The notebooks distributed to all four players can be thought of as the decentralized *blockchain* similar to the Bitcoin blockchain that stores all transactions in the network.

Start of the Monopoly Game

Let's say the game started on 1 November 2020 at 8:00 a.m. and the following actions took place in the first round of this game:
1. Alice landed on Bob's property and paid Bob 1 BTC.
2. Bob landed on Charlie's property and paid Charlie 5 BTC.
3. Charlie passed Go and received 50 BTC. (Note: Charlie passing Go can be thought of as receiving a *block reward*. More on this later.)
4. Debbie rolled the dice, but did not land on anyone's property.

The round ended after all players have rolled their dice. Now imagine all four players made the same records in their notebooks, and then cross-checked each other to ensure that they all have the same information. The transaction will look like this on each players' notebooks.

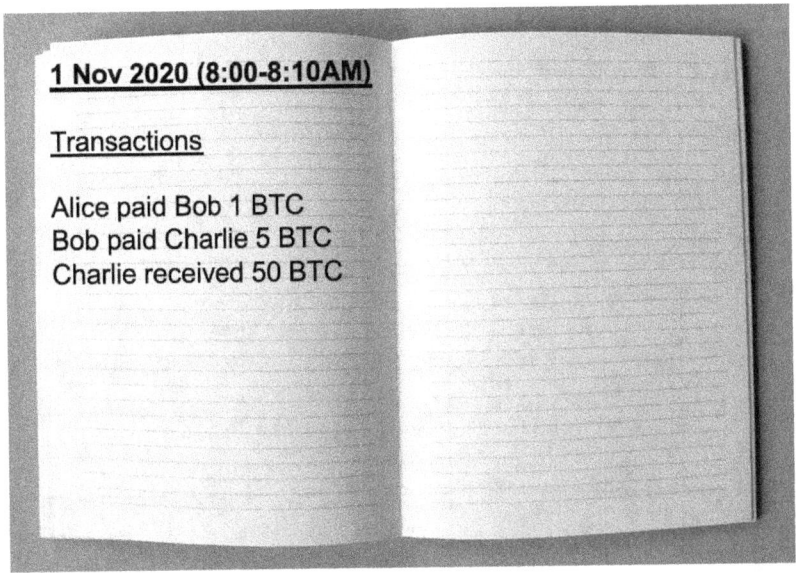

Once everyone has validated that all their transactions tallied with everyone else's, we called it the end of the round. All players have thus reached a *consensus* on the state of all players' balances. The very first page of this notebook is pretty much similar to the first block of the Bitcoin blockchain. At the end of Round 1, we saw the following actions:

Player	Actions
Alice	Landed on Bob's property (*Paid Bob 1 BTC*)
Bob	Landed on Charlie's property (*Paid Charlie 5 BTC*)
Charlie	Passed Go (*Received 50 BTC Block Reward*)
Debbie	No transaction made

The above transactions were recorded on Page 1 of all four players' notebooks. Based on these transaction records, we can then calculate the balances for each player at the end of Round 1.

Player	Balance	Notes
Alice	10 BTC - 1 BTC -------------- 9 BTC --------------	Starting Balance Paid to Bob -------------------------------- End of Round 1 Balance --------------------------------
Bob	10 BTC + 1 BTC - 5 BTC -------------- 6 BTC --------------	Starting Balance Received from Alice Paid to Charlie -------------------------------- End of Round 1 Balance --------------------------------
Charlie	10 BTC + 5 BTC + 50 BTC -------------- 65 BTC --------------	Starting Balance Received from Bob Passed Go (block reward, see below) -------------------------------- End of Round 1 Balance --------------------------------
Debbie	10 BTC -------------- 10 BTC --------------	Starting Balance -------------------------------- End of Round 1 Balance --------------------------------

The table above is a representation of what happened in Round 1. The Monopoly game can keep going on, where each page is effectively similar to a block in a blockchain and contains transactional details. With a record of all transactions taking place, each players' balance can thus be derived at any point in time.

As the game (blockchain) progresses, more payments (transactions) are made, and with each round, a new page (block) is created by players (users).

How are the Pages Generated?

In this Monopoly game, the one thing that was not explained is the 50 BTC block reward that Charlie received. The action of flipping over to a new page is similar to the action of mining and generating a new block.

To fully understand that, it is imperative to first understand how the blockchain works. This may sound a little daunting, but we have made some visualizations to help explain the concept in the following section.

Understanding the Blockchain Structure

In the above Monopoly analogy, we have introduced how transactions are recorded on a blockchain. A quick recap:

1. **Monopoly game** – simulates the **economy** where people transact with one another.

2. **Notebook** – simulates the **blockchain** which contains a record of every transaction. Additionally, each participant will have a copy of the notebook (blockchain).

Blockchain is called the way it is because it is quite literally a series of blocks chained together, in which each block contains transaction data. In this section, we will dig into the structure of a blockchain to illustrate how it works and what makes it tamper-resistant.

However, before we look into what goes inside a blockchain, it is important to understand the concept of a hash function.

In the following sections, we will be looking into what makes up a blockchain, starting with the chain part of it—which are essentially hash functions.

The Chains of a Blockchain – Hash Functions

A hash function converts an input into a fixed-length output of random letters and numbers. This hash function will return the same output given the exact same input. Bitcoin uses the SHA-256 hashing algorithm, which is also used by the US government to protect certain sensitive information.

Hashes made through the SHA-256 algorithm are effectively one-way, which means that given an input (transaction data, block headers etc.), you will be able to produce an output (the resulting hash). However, using the output (the resulting hash), it would not be possible to back-calculate the initial input.

An analogy that can be used to understand how hashing works is to guess the mathematical equation that will result in an answer of 100. For example, some possible equations that will result in 100 are as follow:

1. $1 * 100 = 100$
2. $10 * 10 = 100$
3. $5 * 20 = 100$
4. ... and so on (impossible to pinpoint the correct answer)

As for the hashes themselves, even the smallest change may result in a completely different output. For example, hashing the text "How to Bitcoin" with the SHA-256 function produces the following output:

f8943d8870b292b2137e0e68d5dbae7562fa7666f60e5b17e3dadbe62fcd00b1

If we change the letter i in Bitcoin to 1, the text "How to B1tcoin" then hashes to:

01a8f0c498a439685cbf6929f988379f2f53d5ca41ee169002fd00af83d43817

We can see that by changing even a single character in the input text, the output is completely changed beyond recognition. Therefore, hash functions are extremely important to blockchains as they can be used to summarize and ensure that information cannot be changed without being noticeable.

The Blocks in a Blockchain

The other component of a blockchain is the block, which is made up of two components:

1. **Block Header** is the summary of an entire block and contains:
    a. Hash of the previous block's header,
    b. Hash of all transactions of the current block,
    c. Timestamp – Timestamp the block is "mined" in UNIX
    d. Version – Bitcoin software version
    e. Nonce – Counters used by miners to generate a correct hash
    f. Block difficulty target – difficulty target of the block

    Note that (c) to (f) are like "identification" documents of each block. We will go through them in more detail in later sections.

2. **Block Body** – contains records of all transactions included in the block.

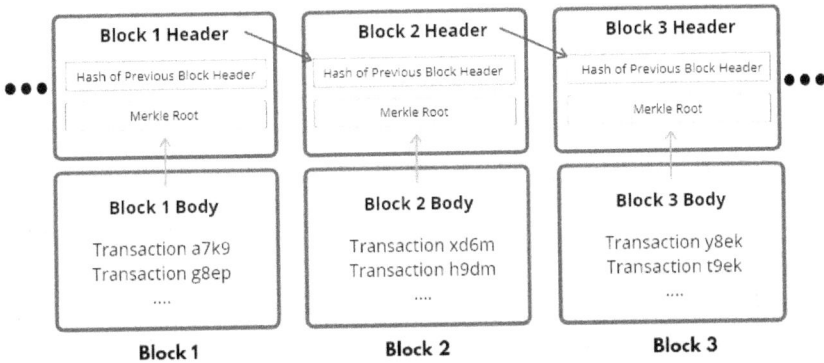

In each block, the list of transactions are all hashed indirectly through the Merkle Root, and included in the block header, such that even 1,000 transactions in the entire body can be represented as a single line of hash. The block header is essentially the "summary" of an entire block, plus a reference to the previous block.

Merkle Root
The merkle root is effectively the hash of all the hashes of all the transactions in a block. In each block, there can be thousands of transactions—the Merkle Root is the hash of all these transactions.

This is an extremely efficient method of storing and verifying transaction data. Merkle root allows one to easily check that a transaction has indeed been verified without needing to go through the entire list of transactions.

Since the Merkle Root is contained in the block header, the block header then effectively contains all information that is required to:
1. Summarize the entire block's transactions (Merkle Root)
2. Link to previous block (contains previous block header's hash)

In the subsequent block, the header of the previous block is hashed, and stored as part of the header of the current block. In this fashion, each block references the previous block using a hash, including the list of all transactions. To change any part of the information in previous blocks, you will have to change everything moving forward as even the most minor change will result in a completely random change of the hash.

Putting it All Together

The Bitcoin ledger makes use of the blockchain technology very effectively. It is a transparent database of transactions distributed globally (the blocks) with tamper-proof features made possible through the use of cryptographic hashing functions (the chain).

So far, we have gone through what makes up a blockchain, but some key details remain missing:

1. What is preventing someone from creating a different version of the entire Bitcoin ledger, and then distributing it as the valid one?
2. What is stopping someone from printing more bitcoin?
3. How do all participants agree on a particular version of the bitcoin ledger at any given time?
4. How are conflicts resolved in the event there are conflicting and different bitcoin ledger versions?

That is where miners come into play. Miners effectively provide security to the Bitcoin network and verify transactions using computers to perform complex mathematical calculations.

Mining on the Blockchain

Before Bitcoin came along, you would basically picture giant tractors, dusty tracks and huge piles of rocks when the term "mining" was mentioned. With the advent of Bitcoin, the term "mining" took a whole new meaning where it refers to the act of solving complex, repetitive computational math problems that can only be effectively done by specialized computers.

The main reason why miners are interested in participating in the Bitcoin mining process is because they are interested in earning the Bitcoin block reward given out to the producer of the next block.

Miners keep the Bitcoin network secure and help everyone stay in sync with one version. They invest electrical energy in the form of computational power to solve complex mathematical problems and are rewarded for their efforts in the form of block rewards. The block reward that miners earn is effectively the fee which the Bitcoin network pays for network security. This method ensures that the Bitcoin blockchain cannot be easily tampered with.

In Bitcoin's case, each block is produced roughly every *10 minutes*. In this 10-minute period, miners pick out transactions to be verified, prioritizing the ones with the highest fees. Once a new block is "mined", transactions that are included are added to the blockchain and broadcasted to participants worldwide—similar to how a new page is used in our Monopoly notebook example earlier.

Here's a handy illustration to showcase the process:

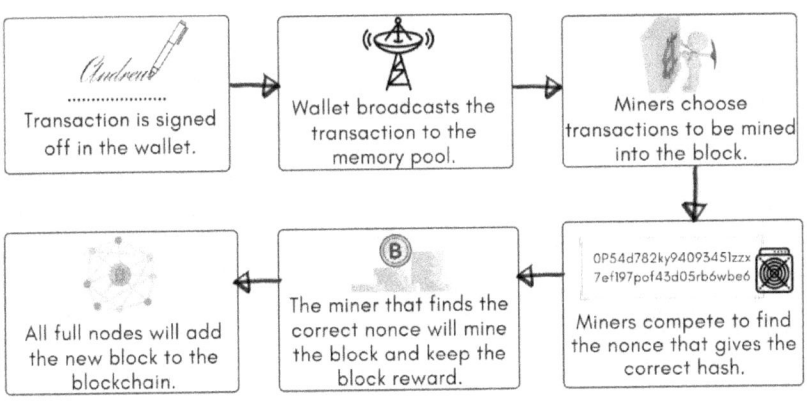

What exactly does a miner do?

In the case of Bitcoin, a miner competes with other miners to find the nonce which gives the correct answer by repeatedly performing SHA-256 hashing calculation. The work done by a miner in finding the solution to this puzzle is also known as the *Proof of Work*.

For each new block, a miner needs to guess an output hash that fulfills a very specific condition—the number of leading zeros. Roughly, the equation is:

Hash output = Hash of (previous block header + merkle root hash + nonce)

The previous block header and Merkle Root hash are known, so miners are effectively guessing the nonce value that will give the correct output hash with a specific number of leading zeros. This is the hash for block number 647,729:

00000000000000000000064b9fcad14d747b725552005db1a77e6344a7c672a9bf

Arriving at the solution above likely requires many iterations and is what makes the mining process computationally expensive. However, one elegant aspect to hashing is that once the input parameters are known, it becomes fairly trivial and easy to verify that it leads to the correct solution. This can be likened to a Sudoku puzzle, whereby it is difficult to solve, but very easy to verify if it is solved correctly.

Bitcoin Mining Machine (or commonly called ASIC)
Bitcoin mining rig is also known as an Application Specific Integrated Circuit (ASIC) machine as it excels at only one thing—calculating SHA-256 hashes for Bitcoin and nothing else.

The power of an ASIC is measured by its hash rate. Hash rate is a measure of how many hashes a machine can compute every second. As of 2020, a retail Bitcoin ASIC can compute around 100 TH/s (12 zeros — that's 100,000,000,000,000 hashes per second). In comparison, a desktop CPU can only calculate in terms of MH/s (6 zeros), orders of magnitude smaller.

Bitcoin Mining Difficulty

Bitcoin mining is often compared to a lottery because it involves luck where miners are required to repetitively guess the solution to a mathematical problem. In Bitcoin's case, miners need to find the nonce as an input to the hash input to guess an output that starts with a required number of zeros (the difficulty).

In a lottery, if you would like to increase your chances of winning, you can buy more lottery tickets. In a similar fashion, miners who want to increase their odds of solving the mathematical puzzle will need to acquire more or faster mining machines.

Miners are granted the block reward when they solve the puzzle for their contribution in securing the network.

As more miners join the network, the likelihood for the network to collectively solve the puzzle and find a block would increase as well. This creates a situation where the solution to the puzzle (and thus a new block) can be found much quicker than 10 minutes.

By design, Bitcoin maintains its 10 minutes block time by maintaining a *difficulty* level—which is the number of zeros required for a solution to be considered valid.

The Bitcoin protocol adjusts the difficulty level every 2,016 blocks (~2 weeks). If the previous 2,016 blocks took less than two weeks to be found, then the difficulty will be increased. If it took more than two weeks, then the difficulty will be reduced. This dynamic adjustment of difficulty ensures that Bitcoin blocks are mined on average once every 10 minutes.

What if two miners find the answers at the same time?

For any given block, the correct nonce that will satisfy the difficulty condition is not limited to just a specific nonce—there are multiple answers. Miners compete with one another to be the first.

This may lead to a situation where two miners find the solution to this mathematical puzzle at the same time. Both miners will broadcast their solutions to the Bitcoin network at the same time where their solutions are considered equally valid by all participants.

In this section, we will go through this scenario briefly to showcase how the Bitcoin protocol handles this situation.

Let's call the two miners Miner A and Miner B. When Miner A and Miner B both discover their respective valid blocks, both miners will announce and propagate their results to the network. Nodes in the network will incorporate the version of the block that they receive first into their blockchain, extending it by one block.

As such nodes that are closest to Miner A will update their blockchain with the latest block being the one announced by Miner A, while nodes that are closest to Miner B will update their blockchain with the latest block being the one announced by Miner B.

Each node will then continue propagating their version of the blockchain to their neighbouring nodes. In this example we have two competing versions of the blockchain that have emerged and we will need a way to resolve this conflict.

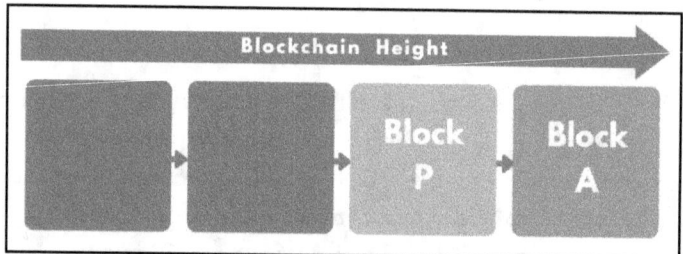

Blockchain Version A

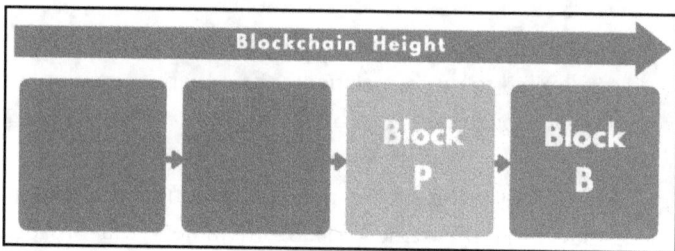

Blockchain Version B

To resolve this conflict and ensure that the blockchain's state remains consistent across all participants in the Bitcoin network, each node will select the blockchain that represents the most Proof of Work, otherwise known as the longest chain.[28]

---

[28] (n.d.). 8. Mining and Consensus - Mastering Bitcoin [Book] – O'Reilly. Retrieved January 20, 2021, from https://www.oreilly.com/library/view/mastering-bitcoin/9781491902639/ch08.html

In this case, miners who added Block A to their blockchain will attempt to find the solution to the next block and build on top of their state of the blockchain. Miners who added Block B to their blockchain will also attempt to find the solution to the next block and build on top of their state of the blockchain.

Eventually, a miner will find a solution and extend the blockchain on either Block A or B. Let's say Miner X next found a solution extending Block B; let's call this Block X. Immediately, Block X forms the longest chain and is thus regarded as the correct state of the blockchain.

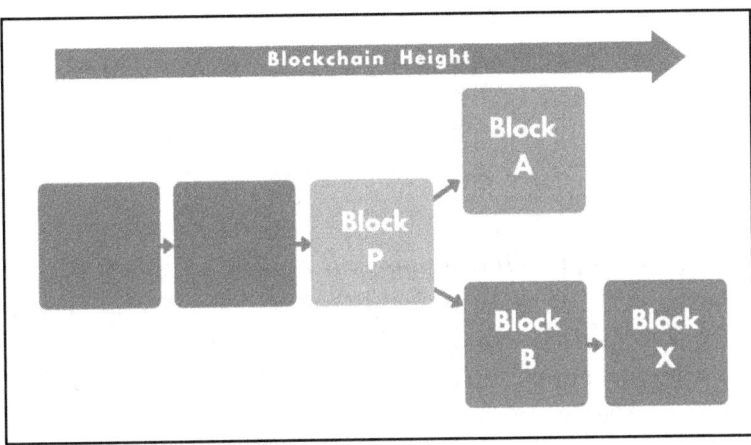

All miners working on finding a solution on top of Block A will stop their work and move on to find a solution to the next puzzle building on top of Block X. Block A is now known as an orphan block. Any transactions in Block A that have not been included in Block B or Block X will now be queued for addition onto the next block on top of Block X.

This is how the Bitcoin protocol deals with the issue of potentially having multiple "versions" of the blockchain.

Bitcoin Transactions

Bitcoin transactions are effectively inputs and outputs on a ledger that is the blockchain. Here's a quick visualization of two common types of transactions:

1. **Payment with change** – Bob has a single address that contains 0.5 BTC. Bob sends 0.1 BTC to Alice, and receives 0.4 BTC as change. This is like paying for coffee with cash using a large banknote and receiving change on it.

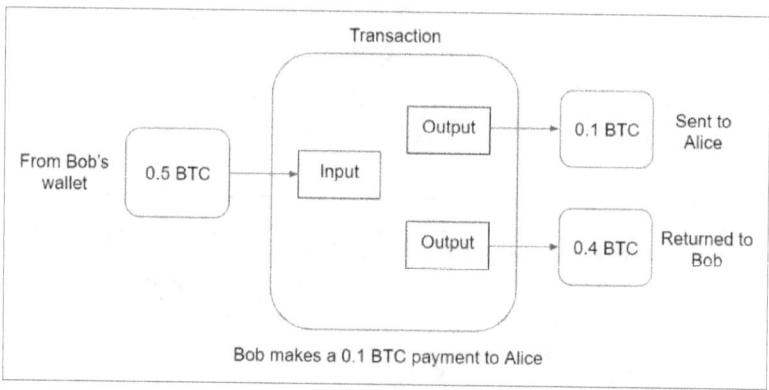

Bob makes a 0.1 BTC payment to Alice

2. **Aggregating multiple inputs into a single payment** – Bob wants to pay 0.7 BTC to Alice and has two separate addresses containing 0.5 BTC each. The balances of the addresses are combined to form a single output of 0.7 BTC to Alice, and Bob receives the remaining 0.3 BTC as change. This is like paying for a large transaction in cash by combining multiple small banknotes to meet the required payment amount.

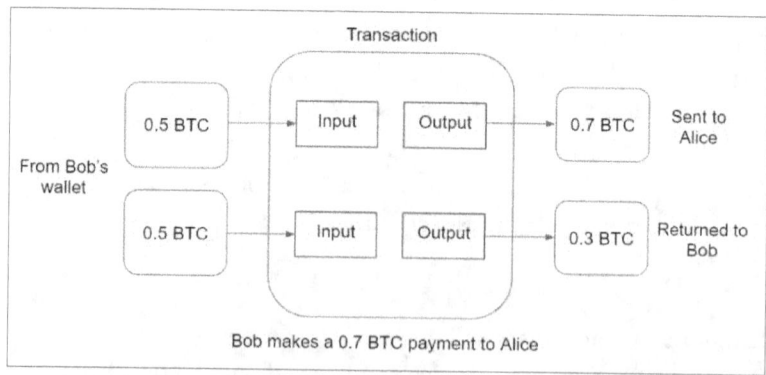

Bob makes a 0.7 BTC payment to Alice

There are many more ways transactions can happen on the Bitcoin blockchain, but the examples above are the most common form of transactions. Knowing how it works will be instrumental in understanding how the Bitcoin protocol handles balances on its ledger.

Note that in the examples above, fees paid to the miners to process the transaction is omitted for simplicity. The fees will go to a different address owned by the miner.

Unspent Transaction Output (UTXO)

Bitcoin transactions are made of inputs and outputs. Unspent transaction outputs, or UTXOs, are exactly what they sound like—they are outputs of blockchain transactions that have not been spent and can be used as inputs for new transactions.

On a fundamental level, UTXOs dictate the beginning and end of each transaction.[29] Whenever a transaction is made, users make use of the balance of UTXOs that they have as inputs. Their digital signature is required to verify that they are the real owners of the inputs, before they are converted into outputs.[30]

After the transaction is completed and added to the blockchain, the UTXOs used as inputs are now considered 'spent', and cannot be used for further actions. However, the transactions create new UTXOs from the resulting outputs, which can be spent later.

How does Bitcoin Prevent Double-Spending?

Double-spending occurs when a malicious user is able to send their bitcoin to two different recipients at the same time.[31] This means the second transaction uses the same input as another transaction and both transactions are relayed to the Bitcoin network at the same time.

Double-spending is a problem unique to digital currencies because digital information can be easily replicated similar to how music and movies can be easily pirated.

---

[29] (2020, June 30). UTXO Definition – Investopedia. Retrieved November 27, 2020, from https://www.investopedia.com/terms/u/utxo.asp

[30] (n.d.). Unspent Transaction Output (UTXO) | Binance Academy. Retrieved November 27, 2020, from https://academy.binance.com/en/glossary/unspent-transaction-output-utxo

[31] (n.d.). Vocabulary – Bitcoin.org. Retrieved January 20, 2021, from https://bitcoin.org/en/vocabulary

Double-spending is not possible when it comes to physical currencies. If you purchase a doughnut for $1, you will have to give that $1 note away to the cashier to receive the doughnut. It is not possible to simultaneously use the same $1 note a second time to purchase coffee too. If you tried to replicate the same $1 note using a photocopy machine, the cashier will immediately be able to know that the photocopied $1 note is not authentic and is able to reject it too.

There are two primary ways to solve the double-spending problem for digital currencies—central clearing counterparty and blockchain.[32] A central clearing counterparty requires trust in a third-party and is the primary way how our traditional financial system works. Bitcoin relies on a blockchain to prevent double-spending from occurring without the need for any centralized authority.

When it comes to people trying to spent bitcoin in a UTXO that has already been spent, say 1 day ago, it is fairly trivial for a miner to check that this is not a valid transaction because this UTXO has already been used as an input to another transaction that has been included in a previous block. As the UTXO was spent 1 day ago, this UTXO would have been included roughly 144 blocks previously.

If the miner insists on allowing this UTXO to be spent and wants to invalidate the earlier transaction, the miner will need to redo all the Proof of Work that has been done for all the previous 144 blocks and race against time to compete against all other miners to create the longest chain. This is computationally very expensive and is thus very improbable.

What if Miners Collude to Double-Spend?

Technically this can happen. Double-spending can occur if a majority of the miners are dishonest. This is known as a 51% attack. This occurs when a single entity is able to control more than 50% of the entire Bitcoin mining capacity. When this occurs, the entity will have enough mining power to modify the ordering of transactions and even exclude certain transactions.

---

[32] (n.d.). Double-Spending – Corporate Finance Institute. Retrieved January 20, 2021, from https://corporatefinanceinstitute.com/resources/knowledge/other/double-spending/

An attacker that has 51% control of a blockchain may double-spend a bitcoin by sending two transactions at the same time to two different addresses. This attack usually targets cryptocurrency exchanges as the value of the attack is the highest. To execute this attack, the first transaction is sent to a merchant to purchase an item and this transaction is broadcasted to the broader Bitcoin network.

The second transaction is sent to the attacker's own address and the attacker will secretly mine another branch of the blockchain that includes the second transaction but not the first transaction. The attacker will continue mining the secret chain for a few blocks until it is longer than the public chain and the first transaction has been accepted by the merchant.

Once this has been done, the secret chain will be broadcasted to the network. As the secret chain is now longer than the public chain, the network will regard the secret chain to be the legitimate chain of the network. The first payment to the merchant will thus be invalidated.

This is one of the reasons why Bitcoin transactions usually require 3 to 6 confirmations by merchants before it is accepted as a valid transaction. The more blocks that have been mined on top of the existing blockchain (each block represents one confirmation), the higher the likelihood that the transaction would not be reversed as more computational power will be needed to complete the Proof of Work needed in adding blocks to the blockchain.

As long as a majority of miners are honest, it will be impossible for any one entity to accumulate 51% of the hashrate and execute this double-spend attack. Bitcoin's network is sufficiently decentralized that no single entity controls 51% of the hashrate.

CHAPTER 3: THE HISTORY OF BITCOIN

Since the inception of the Bitcoin blockchain on 3 Jan 2009, Bitcoin has gone through numerous notable events.

This chapter will discuss several of those events and how they played a role in Bitcoin's developments. A lot has happened, so we will be narrowing it down to some of the most important ones to get you up to speed quickly.

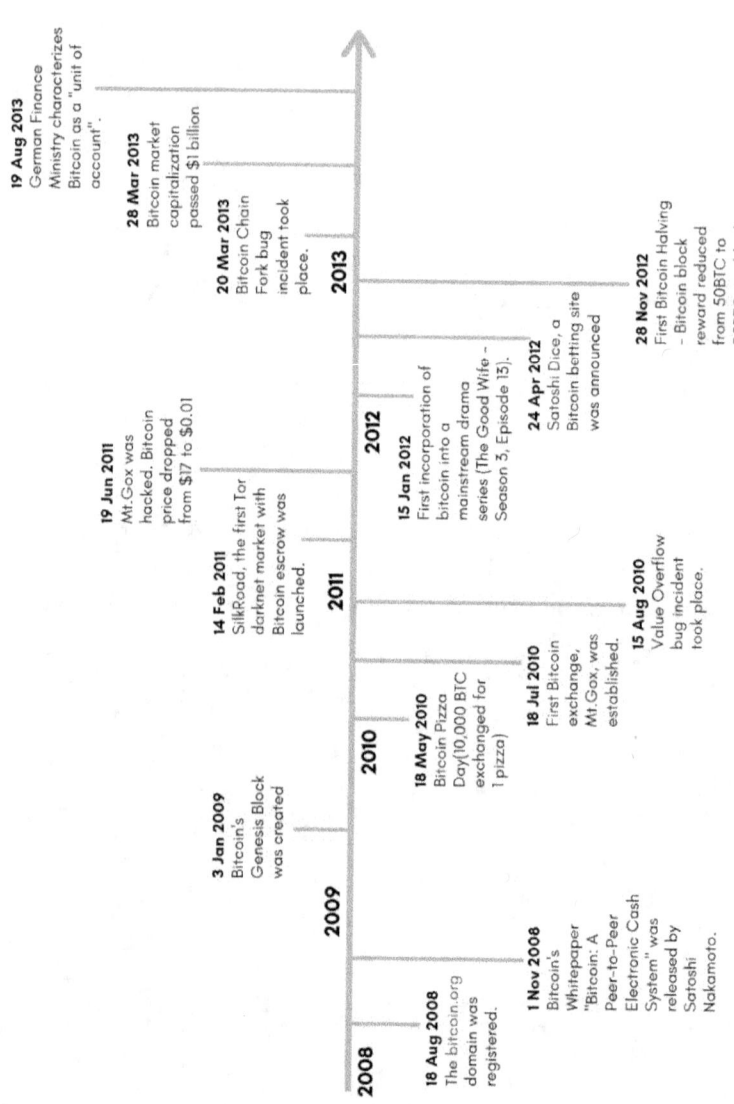

18 Aug 2008
The bitcoin.org domain was registered.

1 Nov 2008
Bitcoin's Whitepaper "Bitcoin: A Peer-to-Peer Electronic Cash System" was released by Satoshi Nakamoto.

2009

3 Jan 2009
Bitcoin's Genesis Block was created

2010

18 May 2010
Bitcoin Pizza Day (10,000 BTC exchanged for 1 pizza)

18 Jul 2010
First Bitcoin exchange, Mt.Gox, was established.

15 Aug 2010
Value Overflow bug incident took place.

2011

14 Feb 2011
SilkRoad, the first Tor darknet market with Bitcoin escrow was launched.

19 Jun 2011
Mt.Gox was hacked. Bitcoin price dropped from $17 to $0.01

2012

15 Jan 2012
First incorporation of bitcoin into a mainstream drama series (The Good Wife - Season 3, Episode 13).

24 Apr 2012
Satoshi Dice, a Bitcoin betting site was announced

28 Nov 2012
First Bitcoin Halving - Bitcoin block reward reduced from 50BTC to 25BTC per block.

2013

20 Mar 2013
Bitcoin Chain Fork bug incident took place.

28 Mar 2013
Bitcoin market capitalization passed $1 billion

19 Aug 2013
German Finance Ministry characterizes Bitcoin as a "unit of account".

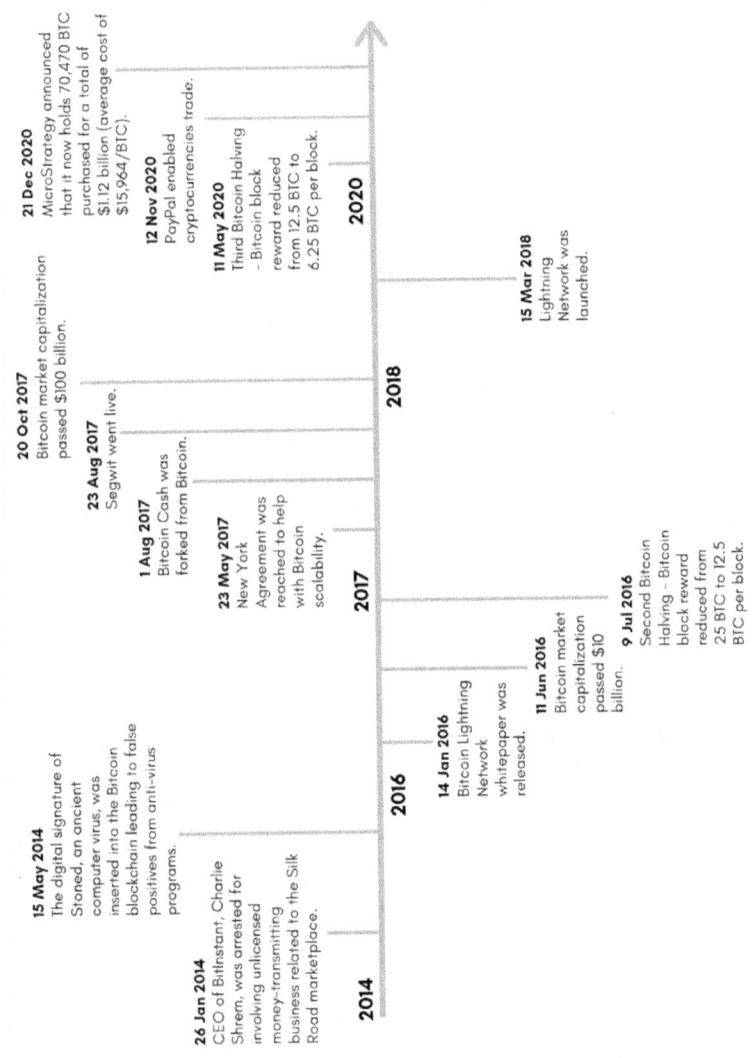

26 Jan 2014
CEO of BitInstant, Charlie Shrem, was arrested for involving unlicensed money-transmitting business related to the Silk Road marketplace.

15 May 2014
The digital signature of Stoned, an ancient computer virus, was inserted into the Bitcoin blockchain leading to false positives from anti-virus programs.

14 Jan 2016
Bitcoin Lightning Network whitepaper was released.

11 Jun 2016
Bitcoin market capitalization passed $10 billion.

9 Jul 2016
Second Bitcoin Halving – Bitcoin block reward reduced from 25 BTC to 12.5 BTC per block.

23 May 2017
New York Agreement was reached to help with Bitcoin scalability.

1 Aug 2017
Bitcoin Cash was forked from Bitcoin.

23 Aug 2017
Segwit went live.

20 Oct 2017
Bitcoin market capitalization passed $100 billion.

15 Mar 2018
Lightning Network was launched.

11 May 2020
Third Bitcoin Halving – Bitcoin block reward reduced from 12.5 BTC to 6.25 BTC per block.

12 Nov 2020
PayPal enabled cryptocurrencies trade.

21 Dec 2020
MicroStrategy announced that it now holds 70,470 BTC purchased for a total of $1.12 billion (average cost of $15,964/BTC).

2014
2016
2017
2018
2020

Bitcoin Key Events

Timeline	Key Events
18 Aug 2008	The bitcoin.org domain was registered
1 Nov 2008	Bitcoin's whitepaper "Bitcoin: A Peer-to-Peer Electronic Cash System" was released by Satoshi Nakamoto
3 Jan 2009	Bitcoin's Genesis Block was created
18 May 2010	Bitcoin Pizza Day (10,000 BTC exchanged for 1 pizza)
18 Jul 2010	First Bitcoin exchange, Mt. Gox, was established
15 Aug 2010	Value Overflow bug incident took place
14 Feb 2011	SilkRoad, the first Tor darknet market with Bitcoin escrow was launched
19 Jun 2011	Mt. Gox was hacked. Bitcoin price dropped from $17 to $0.01
15 Jan 2012	First incorporation of bitcoin into a mainstream drama series (The Good Wife – Season 3, Episode 13)
24 Apr 2012	Satoshi Dice, a Bitcoin betting site was announced
28 Nov 2012	First Bitcoin Halving—Bitcoin block reward reduced from 50 BTC to 25 BTC per block
20 Mar 2013	Bitcoin Chain Fork bug incident took place
28 Mar 2013	Bitcoin market capitalization passed $1 billion
19 Aug 2013	German Finance Ministry characterizes Bitcoin as a "unit of account"
26 Jan 2014	CEO of BitInstant, Charlie Shrem was arrested for unlicensed money-transmitting related to the Silk Road marketplace
15 May 2014	The digital signature of Stoned, an ancient computer virus, was inserted into the Bitcoin blockchain leading to false positives from anti-virus programs
14 Jan 2016	Bitcoin Lightning Network whitepaper was released
11 Jun 2016	Bitcoin market capitalization passed $10 billion

Timeline	Key Events
9 Jul 2016	Second Bitcoin Halving—Bitcoin block reward reduced from 25 BTC to 12.5 BTC per block
23 May 2017	New York Agreement was reached to help with Bitcoin scalability
1 Aug 2017	Bitcoin Cash was forked from Bitcoin
23 Aug 2017	SegWit went live
20 Oct 2017	Bitcoin market capitalization passed $100 billion
15 Mar 2018	Lightning Network was launched
11 May 2020	Third Bitcoin Halving—Bitcoin block reward reduced from 12.5 BTC to 6.25 BTC per block
12 Nov 2020	PayPal enabled cryptocurrencies trade
21 Dec 2020	MicroStrategy announced that it now holds 70,470 BTC purchased for a total of $1.12 billion (average cost of $15,964/BTC)

The above are some of the key events that have transpired in Bitcoin's history. For this chapter, we will be focusing on some of these key events.

The Mt. Gox Hacking

On 19 June 2011, a malicious entity managed to penetrate security measures of the largest Bitcoin exchange at that time—Mt. Gox. A stream of suspicious trades followed soon after, causing the price of bitcoin to plummet from $17 to $0.01.[33]

This allegedly occurred as the attacker was able to access a computer belonging to a Mt. Gox auditor and subsequently transferred the bitcoins illegally to himself or herself. Using the exchange's trading software, the

---

[33] (2011, June 19). Bitcoin prices plummet on hacked exchange | Ars Technica. Retrieved December 4, 2020, from https://arstechnica.com/tech-policy/2011/06/bitcoin-price-plummets-on-compromised-exchange/

attacker sold the stolen bitcoins on the market, creating a large sell order which crashed the price.

However, the price soon corrected to its usual price range within minutes. During the attack, the hacker withdrew $2,000 worth of bitcoin and also leaked Mt. Gox's database, containing the username and encrypted passwords of all the users.[34] Accounts with a total equivalent of close to $9 million were affected by the attack.

To prove that Mt. Gox had the situation under control, more than 400,000 bitcoins were moved from "cold storage" to a Mt. Gox address. Additionally, Mt. Gox attempted to recover from the attack by rolling back all transactions to its previous state before the sell orders were placed.[35]

However, the damage was already done. Soon after this incident, users started facing withdrawal issues. On 28 February 2014, Mt. Gox filed for bankruptcy, claiming that it had lost approximately 850,000 bitcoins, valued at $450 million at the time of filing.

Silk Road Shutdown

In its early days, bitcoin was often associated with illegal purchases as it was perceived to be anonymous, despite this being not quite true. Owing to that, bitcoin became popular as the currency of choice on Silk Road, a darknet marketplace where users can buy and sell illicit substances such as drugs.

Bitcoin is only pseudonymous, meaning someone can still track you as the address owner if they have adequate information. Users of Silk Road who paid and received bitcoin can be tracked down by relevant enforcement agencies with sufficient effort. On 23 June 2013, the Drug Enforcement Administration (DEA) seized a little over 11 bitcoins from one of the

---

[34] (2018, June 20). The Mt. Gox Hack— What's in your Bitcoin Wallet? – Medium. Retrieved December 4, 2020, from https://medium.com/dataseries/the-rise-and-fall-of-mt-gox-whats-in-your-bitcoin-wallet-bd5eb4106f4e

[35] (2011, June 19). Bitcoin collapses on malicious trade • The Register. Retrieved December 18, 2020, from
https://www.theregister.com/2011/06/19/bitcoin_values_collapse_again/

platform's identified sellers, worth approximately $814 dollars at the time of seizure.[36]

However, that amount was measly compared to a bust on a previous drug seller on Silk Road in November 2020 by the US Department of Justice. In this bust, over 70,000 bitcoins worth more than a $1 billion were seized.[37]

Silk Road was shut down when its pseudonymous founder "Dread Pirate Roberts" also known as Ross Ulbricht, was arrested by the Federal Bureau of Investigation (FBI) in October 2013. Although Silk Road became a stain in Bitcoin's history, it served as an example for real-world usage, proving that a decentralized currency could in fact function as a global currency in a barrierless marketplace.

Block Reward Halving

Bitcoin's block reward halving is one of the most notable events in Bitcoin's history. Halving is the process where the block rewards given to miners for successfully mining each block is cut in half.[38]

Block rewards are halved every 210,000 blocks, or roughly every 4 years. The first block reward halving took place at block 210,000 on 28 November 2012, halving the block reward from 50 to 25 BTC per block. The second block reward halving happened on block 420,000 on 9 July 2016, further halving the block reward to 12.5 BTC per block. The third halving took place on block 630,000 on 11 May 2020. At the time of writing (November 2020), we are in the third halving era where 6.25 BTC is distributed each block.

[36] (2013, June 27). The DEA Seized Bitcoins In A Silk Road Drug Raid .... Retrieved December 4, 2020, from https://techcrunch.com/2013/06/27/the-dea-seized-bitcoins-in-a-silk-road-drug-raid/

[37] (2020, November 5). DOJ says it seized over $1 billion in bitcoin from the Silk Road .... Retrieved January 20, 2021, from https://techcrunch.com/2020/11/05/justice-department-silk-road-billion-bitcoin/

[38] (n.d.). Bitcoin halving 2020: research and data for ... – CoinDesk. Retrieved November 10, 2020, from https://www.coindesk.com/crypto-investment-research/bitcoin-halving-2020-research-report

The process of halving will continue every 210,000 blocks until all 21 millions bitcoins have been mined completely. At the time of writing, over two-thirds of all bitcoins, or roughly 18 million bitcoins have been mined.

The following chart shows Bitcoin's block reward schedule and its total supply as it gets towards the maximum supply of 21 million bitcoin in the year 2140.

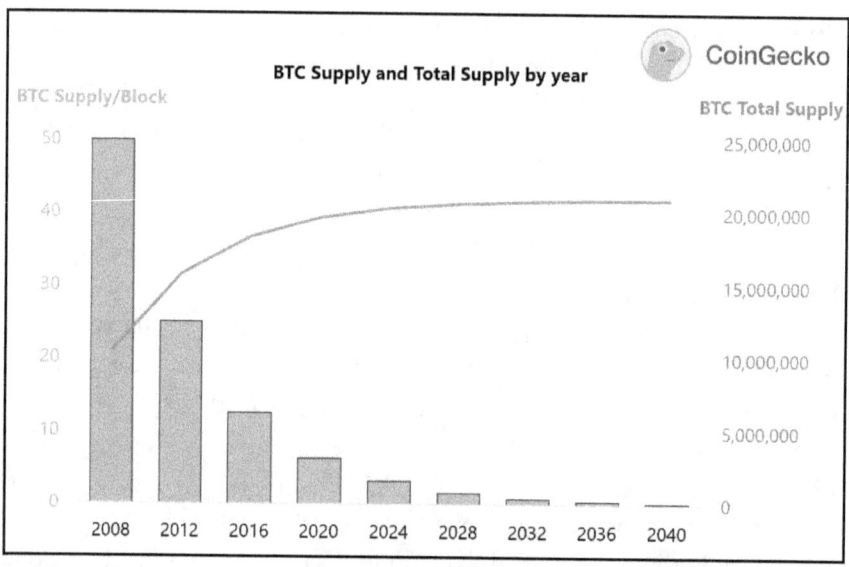

The next block reward halving at block 840,000 will see the block reward reduce from 6.25 to 3.125 BTC per block. This is expected to take place sometime in late May 2024.[39] The exact date and time is still not determined as the Bitcoin block time may vary due to its difficulty level and the chance involved with mining.

Every four years, the Bitcoin community comes together to celebrate this halving event. There is a lot of excitement surrounding the halving event as it represents the growing scarcity of bitcoin. When the block reward halves, the inflation in the Bitcoin ecosystem halves as well.

---

[39] (n.d.). Bitcoin Halving Countdown – CoinGecko. Retrieved November 25, 2020, from https://www.coingecko.com/en/explain/bitcoin_halving

Even though the monetary supply for Bitcoin is known where there is a maximum of 21 million bitcoins, the perception that there are now less bitcoins being emitted each block usually results in a lot of price action during the periods leading up to the block halving event.

New York Agreement (NYA)

Each block in Bitcoin is limited to 1 megabyte (MB) and can only fit a limited number of transactions (approximately 250 byte each). Therefore, the limited throughput is about **3 transactions per second**.

As bitcoin continued to grow rapidly, there was an urgent need for the Bitcoin network to handle more transactions per second. The Bitcoin community endured many months of debates in 2015 and 2016 on the best way to move forward as each suggested scaling solution is not without drawbacks.

Finally, in an attempt to resolve Bitcoin's scaling issues, Barry Silbert, CEO of Digital Currency Group led over 50 Bitcoin companies to jointly propose the New York Agreement on 23 May 2017.[40] The proposal aims to find a workable solution to move Bitcoin forward, but also included some controversial points which might risk causing a rift in the Bitcoin community.[41]

The New York Agreement raised two action items:

1. **Implement Segregated Witness (SegWit)**
   SegWit removes some data from each transaction, which allows for more transactions to be packed into each block. Having more transactions in each block has the added benefit of making transactions cheaper.

---

[40] (2017, June 20). Bitcoin Miners Are Signaling Support for the New York .... Retrieved January 19, 2021, from https://bitcoinmagazine.com/articles/miners-are-signaling-support-new-york-agreement-heres-what-means

[41] (2017, June 27). The Risks of Segregated Witness: Possible Problems Under .... Retrieved November 10, 2020, from https://www.coindesk.com/the-risks-of-bitcoins-segregated-witness-problems-under-us-contract-law

However, opponents claim that SegWit contradicts the very definition of bitcoin as "a chain of digital signatures" as it creates issues for senders and receivers to prove the authenticity of a transaction in the future.

Note: A more in depth explanation for SegWit is available in Chapter 8.

2. **Increase block size to 2 MB**
   By increasing block size, one can pack more data (and therefore more transactions) in each block, effectively increasing Bitcoin network's throughput.

   On the opposite camp, opponents argue that increasing the block size to 2 MB could inflate mining costs because larger blocks will require better mining hardware, thus skewing power away from individual miners to more centralized conglomerates. This goes against the core tenets of Bitcoin which encourages decentralization.

The Bitcoin community voted on the New York Agreement after debating and weighing the pros and cons of each solution. They ultimately reached a majority consensus to deploy SegWit and improve block capacity despite the potential risks. On 24 August 2017, SegWit was successfully included in the Bitcoin protocol and the throughput for the Bitcoin network increased to 7 TPS.

However, the second part of the New York Agreement, which is to increase the block size to 2 MB did not succeed. This ultimately divided and split the community and led to a hard fork of Bitcoin, resulting in Bitcoin Cash.

Lightning Network
Bitcoin's network (post SegWit) can only handle 7 transactions per second and requires 10 minutes to finalize—simply insufficient as a global payments system. It is also a far cry compared to Visa's payment network which can handle approximately 24,000 transactions per second. To solve this issue, the Lightning Network was proposed as a potential solution.

Lightning Network is effectively a second layer payment channel built on top of the Bitcoin network which records transactions on a separate sidechain that is still verifiable on the main Bitcoin network.[42] It achieves several key goals:

1. **High throughput** – Lightning Network has a theoretical throughput of 1 million transactions per second (vs. 7 transactions per second for Bitcoin)
2. **Fast transactions** – Transactions are processed in under a minute (vs. 10 minutes for Bitcoin main network)
3. **Low fees** – Fees on Lightning Network are much lower and almost negligible (vs. fees on the main Bitcoin network)
4. **Reduces congestion** – Once adopted, Lightning Network can potentially reduce traffic on the main Bitcoin blockchain as payments primarily get processed on the Lightning Network sidechain

Lightning Network is still in its early stage and is not entirely bug-free. Teams such as ACINQ, Blockstream, and Lightning Labs are still hard at work developing Lightning Network further.

Note: A more in-depth explanation for Lightning Network is available in Chapter 8.

Bugs

The Bitcoin protocol is software written by humans and mistakes are bound to happen within the codebase itself. On two separate occasions, bugs were found on the Bitcoin codebase and caused major disruption to the protocol.

In both cases, Bitcoin developers and community members rallied together to rectify the bugs and keep the protocol running smoothly. An interesting statistic to note for Bitcoin is that it has reported a 99.986% server uptime[43], which is comparable to an enterprise-grade service provider's guarantee for servers such as Amazon Web Services.

---

[42] (n.d.) What Is Lightning Network And How It Works – Cointelegraph. Retrieved November 17, 2020, from https://cointelegraph.com/lightning-network-101/what-is-lightning-network-and-how-it-works

[43] (n.d.). 99.98% – Bitcoin Uptime Tracker (Updated Live). Retrieved November 26, 2020, from https://www.buybitcoinworldwide.com/bitcoin-uptime/

Value Overflow Incident (15 August 2010)

The value overflow bug was one of the biggest bugs that had been found in Bitcoin.[44] Without a proper solution, it would ruin Bitcoin. The incident happened because the code for checking Bitcoin transactions did not work if outputs were so large that they overflowed when summed.[45]

One hacker took advantage of this bug and generated 184 billion bitcoins out of thin air. Remember, Bitcoin's total supply was set to be capped at 21 million.

Jeff Garzig, a former Bitcoin Core developer spotted the anomaly and reported on the Bitcointalk forum.[46] Satoshi took the matter seriously and within 3 hours, released a Bitcoin software upgrade to version 0.3.10. The software upgrade reseted the Bitcoin blockchain and removed the abnormal transaction that generated 184 billion bitcoins out of thin air.

This software upgrade did not solve the issue entirely yet because now, there are two blockchains running—the older blockchain with the abnormal transaction and the updated blockchain that did not contain the abnormal transaction.

Miners were informed about the incident and were urged to upgrade their software to mine the new chain and stop mining the bad chain. After 19 hours, the good chain became the dominant chain and many miners stopped mining the bad chain altogether. This finally put an end to the value overflow incident and maintained Bitcoin's integrity.

Chain Fork Incident (20 March 2013)

The chain fork incident occurred when Bitcoin was trying to upgrade from version 0.7 to version 0.8.[47] This update was intended to replace a database library software in the Bitcoin codebase from Berkeley DB to LevelDB.

---

[44] (2016, July 22). Value overflow incident – Bitcoin Wiki. Retrieved November 10, 2020, from https://en.bitcoin.it/wiki/Value_overflow_incident

[45] (2019, January 11). Bitcoin's Biggest Hack In History: 184.4 Billion ... – Hacker Noon. Retrieved January 20, 2021, from https://hackernoon.com/bitcoins-biggest-hack-in-history-184-4-ded46310d4ef

[46] (2010, August 16). Strange block 74638 – Bitcoin Forum. Retrieved November 10, 2020, from https://bitcointalk.org/index.php?topic=822.0

During the software upgrade, the Bitcoin developers accidentally removed an unknown 10,000 database lock limit in the new version 0.8. As a result, blocks created in version 0.8 contained unusually large amounts of transactions that were not compatible with version 0.7.

The incompatibility caused the Bitcoin blockchain to split with miners on version 0.7 rejecting the abnormal new blocks on version 0.8 and forming its own new blockchain.

Fortunately, the chain split was detected very quickly. Two major mining pools, BTCGuild and Slush, took the lead to downgrade their mining software to the older version 0.7 despite potential losses in revenue. With most miners downgrading back to version 0.7 soon after, the chain split was soon resolved in 6 hours and 20 minutes.

Immediately after the incident, version 0.8.1 was released to fix the bugs on version 0.8 with some additional rules. The rules set the block size limits to 500,000 bytes and rejected blocks with more than 10,000 locks. Miners were then urged to upgrade and mine on version 0.8.1, which had the new standardized rules.

Fun Fact

As of time of writing, Bitcoin has been declared dead 393 times.[48] Despite the numerous times various figures and media calling Bitcoin dead, it has yet to happen.

You can track bitcoin's 'death' at Bitcoin Obituary, a satire website which collects and aggregates news articles and blogs that announced bitcoin as "dead".

---

[47] (n.d.). bips/bip-0050.mediawiki at master · bitcoin/bips · GitHub. Retrieved November 10, 2020, from https://github.com/bitcoin/bips/blob/master/bip-0050.mediawiki
[48] (n.d.). Bitcoin Obituaries - Bitcoin Declared Dead 350+ ... – 99Bitcoins. Retrieved January 20, 2021, from https://99bitcoins.com/bitcoin-obituaries/

PART 2: BITCOIN & YOU

CHAPTER 4: KEEPING YOUR BITCOINS SAFE

This chapter will go through the various types of Bitcoin wallets and the steps needed to keep your bitcoins safe and sound. When you store your fiat currencies in your bank account, the bank is responsible for storing those funds safely. However, when it comes to cryptocurrencies, you are responsible for your own funds.

As the name suggests, a Bitcoin wallet is a software where you can store, send, and receive bitcoins. A Bitcoin wallet helps you with the management of your private and public keys. Private keys are used to sign transactions to send any bitcoin that you own while public keys are derived from the private keys to generate Bitcoin addresses.

Using your email inbox as an analogy, you can think of your Bitcoin private key as the password to your email account and the bitcoin address as the email address to which people can send things to.

There are various intricate and interesting mathematics that goes behind these keys and addresses.[49] However, for the sake of simplicity, here's what you need to know about keys and addresses.

---

[49] (n.d.). 4. Keys, Addresses - Mastering Bitcoin, 2nd Edition ... – O'Reilly. Retrieved December 16, 2020, from https://www.oreilly.com/library/view/mastering-bitcoin-2nd/9781491954379/ch04.html

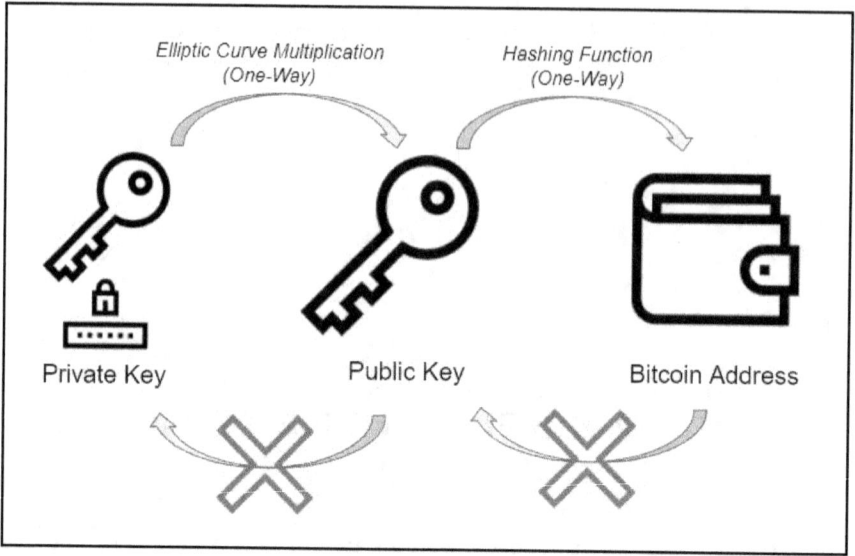

With the private key, one can easily generate a public key.[50] Using the public key, one can then generate a bitcoin address where bitcoins can be sent to. However, doing the reverse is nearly impossible mathematically.

Your private key is something that you must guard closely because this gives access to your entire Bitcoin wallet and balances. Anyone with access to your Bitcoin private key can take your entire bitcoin balance just like how anyone with access to your email password can read all your emails and impersonate you.

Private Key

The private key is used to digitally sign any transactions that will spend one's bitcoin. An example of a Bitcoin private key can be seen below. It contains 64 characters:

a966eb6058f8ec9f47074a2faadd3dab42e2c60ed05bc34d39d6c0e1d32b8bdf

---

[50] (2018, October 22). How to get an address from a private key on Bitcoin – Crypto ....
Retrieved January 20, 2021, from https://www.crypto-lyon.fr/how-to-get-an-address-from-a-private-key-on-bitcoin.html

Bitcoin's public key is mathematically derived from the private key. It is currently close to impossible to use reverse mathematics in order to derive the private key from the public key.

Essentially, creating a bitcoin private key is the same as picking a random number between 1 and 2^{256} (2 multiplied by itself for 256 times). To give you a sense of scale, 2^{256} results in a number that has 78 digits, and on your calculator 2^{256} should look something like:

115,792,089,237,316,195,423,570,985,008,687,907,853,
269,984,665,640,564,039,457,584,007,913,129,639,936

Or, for a more readable one:

1.158×10^{77}
(that's 1.1 with 77 zeros behind)

This is a mind-bogglingly large number. In comparison, if we were to count the seconds since the universe theoretically first began, that number (13.7 billion years[51]) would approximately result in 435,075,697,224,000,000 seconds (or 4.35×10^{17}, nowhere close to 1.158×10^{77}). Another mind-blowing comparison is with another estimate which puts the number of atoms of the observable universe at 10^{80} atoms, that is 1 with 80 zeros behind.

In short, private keys are extremely hard to guess and close to impossible to brute force. The difficulty is likely analogous to choosing a single grain of sand on a beach and later asking a friend to find that exact same grain of sand among all the beaches on earth.

Private keys might be hard to guess, but you can still lose them through other means.

It is important that you absolutely do not reveal your private keys to anyone. Do not upload your private keys to the internet and always have a non-digital backup of your private keys somewhere. Your

---

[51] (n.d.). The Universe By Numbers – The Physics of the Universe. Retrieved January 20, 2021, from https://www.physicsoftheuniverse.com/numbers.html

private keys are used to spend your bitcoin and losing it will result in the loss of your bitcoin forever.

Public Key and Bitcoin Address

Public keys are derived from private keys. It is created by applying elliptic-curve cryptography to the private key.

It is useful to understand that a public key is not the same as your bitcoin address. Public keys, like private keys, are used to generate bitcoin addresses. In fact, a public key can generate multiple bitcoin addresses using the BIP32 Hierarchical Deterministic wallet standard.

Just like private keys, it is recommended that you do not share your Public Key with anyone unless absolutely necessary. Fortunately, a non-technical user will seldom come across the need to know or use public keys. Your bitcoin wallet software will do the technical stuff for you.

You will, however, need to be familiar with the next concept to be a better Bitcoin user—Bitcoin Addresses.

Think of your bitcoin addresses as your computer's IP addresses where the internet can send data to you.[52]

Bitcoin addresses look something like the following:

12rBqcTDCai3MHE3HMie4whkf9X8odffkH

Bitcoin addresses begin with a 1, 3, or bc1 followed by a string of random characters. While all three address types can send and receive bitcoin, it is worth noting the difference among them.

The address type which begins with 1 is known as a P2PKH address. P2PKH stands for Pay-to-Pubkey Hash, which means to pay to a hash of a recipient's public key. This is the original address format for Bitcoin and although they are still in use today, they are considered legacy addresses.

---

[52] (2020, June 23). IP Address Definition – Investopedia. Retrieved January 20, 2021, from https://www.investopedia.com/terms/i/ip-address.asp

These address transactions are larger in size and may incur higher network fees.[53] They are also not compatible with SegWit.

The next address type which starts with 3 is known as a P2SH address, or 'Pay-to-Script Hash' address. P2SH addresses allow for greater functionality compared to P2PKH addresses. The script function in P2SH is most commonly used for multisignature addresses (multisig for short), which requires multiple signatures before a transaction is executed. This address type can be used to send funds to both SegWit and non-SegWit addresses.

The final type of address begins with 'bc1' and is known as a Bech32 address. Bec32 addresses are native SegWit addresses. These SegWit native addresses are naturally more efficient with the use of block space, resulting in lower transaction fees.[54] Bech32 addresses are longer compared to the previous two address types. As it is relatively new, some wallets and exchanges may not accept sending or receiving bitcoins to this address type.

Wallets

Bitcoin wallets can generally be classified into two broad categories, namely hot and cold wallets. There are several types of wallets available within these categories such as mobile, desktop, hardware, and paper wallets.

Although they are called wallets, they basically function like personal bank accounts for your bitcoins where you can transfer and receive bitcoin in your wallets. Wallets are either custodial or non-custodial.

Custodial wallets are wallets which you do not control the private keys. Rather, the private keys are controlled by third parties on your behalf. These wallets are similar to traditional bank accounts where the accounts are in your name but are ultimately controlled by the financial institutions on your behalf. Because the funds are not directly under your control, these institutions may freeze or seize your funds at any time.

---

[53] (2020, January 22). Bitcoin address formats and performance ... – FixedFloat. Retrieved November 25, 2020, from https://fixedfloat.com/blog/guides/bitcoin-address-formats
[54] (2020, October 13). Bech32 – Bitcoin Wiki. Retrieved November 25, 2020, from https://en.bitcoin.it/wiki/Bech32

Non-custodial wallets are wallets where you control the private keys. These are wallets that you have full control over and no one can take your funds away from you without your permission—you are essentially becoming your own bank. Therefore, you must take full responsibility and precautions to secure the funds from thieves and hackers. Losing control of your private keys will most likely mean the loss of all your funds with no recourse.

There are no right or wrong wallets to use when it comes to storing your funds. Each person will have to choose a wallet which he or she is comfortable with and take all precautions to store it safely. It is generally a good idea to split your funds across a few wallets.

We will be going through the differences between all these wallet types. By the end of this chapter, you will get a better idea of the types of wallets that you should use.

Hot Wallets

Hot wallets are cryptocurrency wallets that are connected to the Internet, therefore funds stored in such wallets are much more accessible. However, it is less secure compared to cold wallets as there are more attack vectors available to hackers.

There are two main types of hot wallets available, namely desktop and mobile wallets. As the terms suggest, desktop wallets are available on computers and laptops while mobile wallets are available as apps downloadable on smartphones.

Below, we will go through some of the most popular desktop and mobile wallets.

Desktop Wallets
Full Node Wallets

Bitcoin Core
The first Bitcoin wallet created was a desktop wallet known as Bitcoin Core, previously known as Bitcoin-QT. In order to use it, you have to download the entire Bitcoin blockchain. You would need a large hard disk to use this wallet as the Bitcoin blockchain is currently about 300 GB.[55] Due to the large blockchain size, it may take a few days to download and sync the full blockchain.

Steps to setup a Bitcoin Core wallet is in Chapter 7.

Simple Payment Verification (SPV) Wallets
The large disk space required to download and use Bitcoin Core may prove a hindrance for many. Thus, Simple Payment Verification (SPV) wallets were soon developed. SPV wallets do not require you to download the Bitcoin blockchain. Instead, the state of the blockchain is synced via a remote node. Some SPV wallets which are widely used include Electrum, Exodus, and Atomic Wallet.

Electrum Wallet
Electrum is one of the oldest desktop wallets to exist, supporting multiple operating systems and integration with hardware wallets. In terms of crypto assets, it only supports bitcoin. Electrum allows you to tag addresses, customize transaction fees for each transaction and also provides encryption. Although the user interface is not very beginner-friendly, it is still a decent wallet for amateur and veteran Bitcoiners.

---

[55] (n.d.). Bitcoin blockchain size 2009-2021 | Statista. Retrieved January 20, 2021, from https://www.statista.com/statistics/647523/worldwide-bitcoin-blockchain-size/

Exodus Wallet

With UI built for beginners in mind, Exodus supports more than 30 cryptocurrencies besides bitcoin. For transactions made using the wallet, fees are paid to the network and not to Exodus. Network fees are automatically calculated, but it may cost more than required for the sake of speed.[56] However, security is rather lackluster as it does not support multi-signature addresses and two-factor authentication (2FA).

Atomic Wallet

Supporting over 300 coins and tokens, Atomic Wallets allows users with a diverse portfolio of cryptocurrencies to manage their assets in a single interface. With their Atomic Swap feature, users can exchange between different currencies without going through an exchange. It does not take any fees but network fees are still required for verifying transactions.[57]

Mobile Wallets

Blockchain.com

Blockchain.com is one of the most popular mobile wallet providers. It supports multiple cryptocurrencies and offers Swap, an in-wallet crypto-to-crypto exchange. With up to three tiers of advanced security features and an intuitive UI, Blockchain.com has a high level of privacy and is easy for beginners to use.

Steps to setup a Blockchain.com wallet is in Chapter 6.

---

[56] (2020, September 7). Exodus Wallet Review: What is Exodus? Is ... – BitDegree. Retrieved November 20, 2020, from https://www.bitdegree.org/crypto/exodus-wallet-review

[57] (n.d.). Does Atomic Wallet have fees to send or receive the assets .... Retrieved November 20, 2020, from https://support.atomicwallet.io/article/77-does-atomic-wallet-have-fees-to-send-or-receive-the-assets

Samourai

The Samourai wallet considers itself as a wallet that takes security to another level. It has numerous privacy features such as the "stealth mode" which completely hides any trace of Samourai's existence on your device.[58] However, it only supports Bitcoin and only available on Android devices.

Steps to setup a Samourai wallet is in Chapter 7.

Coinbase Wallet

With support for various cryptocurrencies, digital collectibles and over 50 fiat currencies, it is easy to use and available on most devices. It has two-factor authentication, which boosts security. While network fees remain, there are zero fees for transactions between other Coinbase wallets.[59]

Steps to setup a Coinbase wallet is in Chapter 5.

Cold Wallets

Cold wallets are cryptocurrency wallets that are useful for storing large amounts of Bitcoin. Because they are not connected to the Internet, they are more secure and are harder for hackers to attack.

There are two main types of cold wallets available: hardware and paper wallets. Hardware wallets are physical devices used specifically to store cryptocurrencies, while paper wallets are materials printed with the Bitcoin private keys.

---

[58] (n.d.). Stealth Mode – Samourai Wallet. Retrieved November 22, 2020, from https://samouraiwallet.com/stealth

[59] (n.d.). Coinbase pricing and fees disclosures | Coinbase Help. Retrieved November 22, 2020, from https://help.coinbase.com/en/coinbase/trading-and-funding/pricing-and-fees/fees

Below, we will go through some of the most popular hardware and paper wallets.

Hardware Wallets

A hardware wallet is a physical device solely for storing cryptocurrencies—in this case, bitcoin. Hardware wallets keep private keys separate from internet-connected devices, reducing the chances of your wallet being compromised.

In hardware wallets, the private keys are maintained in a secure offline environment even if it's plugged into a device infected with malware. While hardware wallets can be physically stolen, it is not accessible if the thief doesn't know your passcode. In the unfortunate event that your hardware wallet is damaged or stolen, you will still be able to recover your funds if you had created a secret backup code prior to the loss.

The top manufacturers of hardware wallets at the moment are Ledger and Trezor, though more have been emerging lately. In this book, we will be covering the models produced by Ledger and Trezor.

Hardware wallets can be costly, with prices ranging from $50 to over $300. Some hardware wallets contain a screen, allowing you to check on important wallet details. Below are some of the most popular hardware wallets available for purchase. Note: All prices are correct as of the time of writing.

Ledger Nano S
Made of stainless steel yet still light in weight, the Ledger Nano S supports multiple cryptocurrencies and is compatible with many software wallets and decentralized applications (dApps). Coming in at a price of $59, it is an affordable wallet for beginners and uses a micro USB connection.

Ledger Nano X

Similar to the Nano S, this hardware wallet supports more than 1,500 cryptocurrencies and can store up to 100 applications. The main difference is the Ledger Nano X comes with Bluetooth connectivity, making it even easier to manage your Bitcoin on the go. Unlike the Nano S, it uses a Type-C USB connection. With a price tag of $119, this wallet would be a viable option for future upgrades.

Trezor One

One of the first hardware wallets to exist on the market, the Trezor One is a decent choice for beginners and veterans alike, with support for over 1,000 crypto assets. Built with a different form factor, similar to a car key rather than a thumb drive, it can fit in your pocket with ease. The Trezor One can be used as a two-factor authentication key and uses a micro-USB connection.[60]

Trezor Model T

With a coloured-LCD touchscreen display and a magnetic dock, the Trezor Model T is one of the high-end options available for hardware wallets. It supports more crypto assets compared to the Trezor One and comes with a microSD slot.[61] However, these features do not come cheap. At $170 per unit, it is suitable for more experienced users rather than newcomers.

---

[60] (n.d.). Trezor White – Official Trezor Shop. Retrieved November 23, 2020, from https://shop.trezor.io/product/trezor-one-white

[61] (n.d.). Trezor Model T – Official Trezor Shop. Retrieved November 23, 2020, from https://shop.trezor.io/product/trezor-model-t

Paper Wallets

At its core, paper wallets give you complete ownership and access to your bitcoins. As long as you have the private key to a Bitcoin address, you can move the bitcoin in it. So long as you and no one else owns the private key, you are the rightful owner of the bitcoin.

Paper wallets can easily be passed to friends and family without the need for any computer or software setup. Imagine getting a paper wallet loaded with some bitcoin as a Christmas present. That would be quite a gift!

However, the safekeeping of paper wallets is important—whoever that has access to a paper wallet will be able to take control of any bitcoin stored by moving the bitcoin to a private key that they control.

Paper wallets are best generated on a brand new computer that has not been connected to the Internet. It is not recommended that you use a paper wallet hosted on any website as the website may be compromised and a hacker may then detect your private key and sweep all the bitcoin that is sent to it in the future.

Paper wallets are not recommended in general because you will still need to print the wallet, opening it to another layer of attack by hackers. Any printed paper wallets are also subjected to wear and tear. Imagine waking up one day to discover that your paper wallet has been damaged by insects, water, fire or other natural elements!

Common Bitcoin Risks

When you store money in your bank account, the money is meant to be secured by the bank. Additionally, some governments provide additional guarantees against bank failures with a Federal Deposit Insurance Scheme which insures your money in the bank up to a certain threshold. In the United States, the Federal Deposit Insurance Corporation (FDIC) insures deposits up to $250,000 per depositor on a member financial institution.

However, when it comes to storing bitcoin, you are fully in charge of keeping it safe. While it is possible to store your bitcoins in an exchange or in a custodial wallet (like a bank), there is no guarantee that it will be kept safe. Unfortunately, many hacks have taken place throughout the years.

Here are some of the common risks prevalent in the Bitcoin ecosystem.

Centralized Exchange Hack

When you store your bitcoin on a centralized exchange, you are essentially trusting the exchange to safeguard your bitcoin for you; you do not keep or have access to your private keys. However, this may not be the best idea, especially given the number of hacks that have taken place since the inception of Bitcoin.

The majority of exchanges keep some funds in hot wallets, which are constantly under attack by hackers. The largest hack to have occurred is the infamous Mt. Gox hack in early 2014; it resulted in the loss of 850,000 bitcoins worth approximately $450 million during the time of incident.[62] Since then, multiple other hacks have taken place at other centralized platforms.

Remember this phrase: if it's not your keys, it's not your crypto.

Phishing

Phishing is one of the most common methods used by attackers when attempting to steal bitcoin or other cryptocurrencies.[63] It's a method in

---

[62] (2020, February 10). Mt. Gox: The Story Of The Biggest Ever Bitcoin Hack | Trading .... Retrieved January 20, 2021, from https://trading-education.com/mt-gox-the-story-of-the-biggest-ever-bitcoin-hack

[63] (n.d.). Phishing | What Is Phishing? – Phishing.org. Retrieved January 20, 2021, from

which targets are contacted by an attacker who poses as a representative of an institution. They then attempt to convince the victim to provide confidential information such as private keys, seed phrases, and passwords.

Some things to look out for to avoid being phished are:
1. If the offer is too good to be true, it's likely a scam. One of the more popular ones is: send 1 BTC to this address to receive back 2 BTC.
2. "Project representatives" requesting your private keys or seed phrases in order to help you out with an issue. Representatives of projects will not approach you directly to send funds to an address.
3. Phishing websites. Attackers may copy popular websites with a very similar hyperlink to get their victims to key in sensitive information. Always be sure to double-check the URL before proceeding with it.

The Basics of Bitcoin Security

To better safeguard your bitcoin, it is important for you to practise good security practices. Here are some precautions and steps that you can take.

Password Manager

Hacking incidents amongst online web portals have been occurring with increased frequency in the past few years. In the dark web, hackers frequently sell passwords of online accounts obtained from hacked web portals.

Because most people use the same passwords on multiple online accounts, a breach on one web portal may compromise your accounts at other web portals. For example, if you store bitcoin on a crypto exchange and reuse the same password, it would be easy for a hacker to access your exchange account and withdraw your bitcoins.

You can use the website *Have I Been Pwned* (https://haveibeenpwned.com/) to check if your account has been compromised in a previous hacking incident. In this website, you may see a list of past hacking incidents. If you find your email address listed, it is best to change the password of all the web portals using similar passwords.

---

https://www.phishing.org/what-is-phishing

To minimise your risk, it is a good idea to use different passwords for each online account—if one of these services were hacked, it would not compromise the security of your other online accounts.

Password managers like 1Password or LastPass can help you manage the hundreds of different passwords required for each online account. Not only can they help you generate strong and unique passwords for all your online services, they can also store and encrypt all your unique login information. All you need to remember is one strong master password to access your entire password vault.

Two-Factor Authentication (2FA)

To further increase the security of your online accounts, consider turning on two-factor authentication (2FA) where possible.[64] 2FA is an extra layer of security that one has to undergo during the login process. It usually comes in the form of a 6-digit code generated on a second device, usually your mobile phone.

With 2FA, if a hacker were somehow able to figure out your account username and password, the hacker would still not be able to access your account unless he or she also has your 2FA code, which resets every few seconds. It is highly imperative that you never share your 2FA code with anyone else.

2FA codes can be generated via SMS or an authenticator app like Google Authenticator or Authy. SMS-based 2FA is generally regarded as a weaker form of 2FA as it is subjected to SIM-swap attacks where the hacker will misrepresent himself or herself as you to get your telco company to swap your SIM to a different device so that the hacker can receive the 2FA code.

2FA is compulsory for most exchanges due to the high rates of hacking incidents. Although 2FA adds an extra, inconvenient step during the login process, it helps to secure your account better.

---

[64] (2020, October 15). What is two-factor authentication (2FA) and how does ... – Norton. Retrieved November 26, 2020, from https://us.norton.com/internetsecurity-how-to-importance-two-factor-authentication.html

Remove Unused Browser Extensions

Many web browsers allow you to add features and personalize your browsing experience by installing extensions. On Google Chrome, these small programs are known as Chrome Extensions.

Although Chrome Extensions enhance our web browsing experience, we have to be careful as some of them may be malicious and used by hackers to alter or steal data from your devices. These malicious extensions may be keyloggers or phishing tools designed to steal passwords and private keys.[65]

If it is necessary to use an extension, it is a good idea to install the extension on a different Chrome user profile that is separate from your day-to-day browsing experience. That way, if the extension is malicious, it is tied to one specific Chrome account. It is also useful to review the permissions requested by the extension to ensure what is requested is within the parameters of what is needed to perform its tasks.

Do Not Click on Ads

Numerous phishing websites exist to trick users into visiting them via advertisements on Google, Youtube, Facebook and other popular platforms. Many ads look legitimate but are designed to extract your private keys, allowing hackers to steal your bitcoin.

Here's one example—if you search for Blockchain.com in Google Search, phishing links disguised as ads show up above the real website.

---

[65] (2020, June 18). How hackers used malicious Chrome extensions in a mass .... Retrieved January 20, 2021, from https://www.cyberscoop.com/chrome-spyware-awake-security-galcomm/

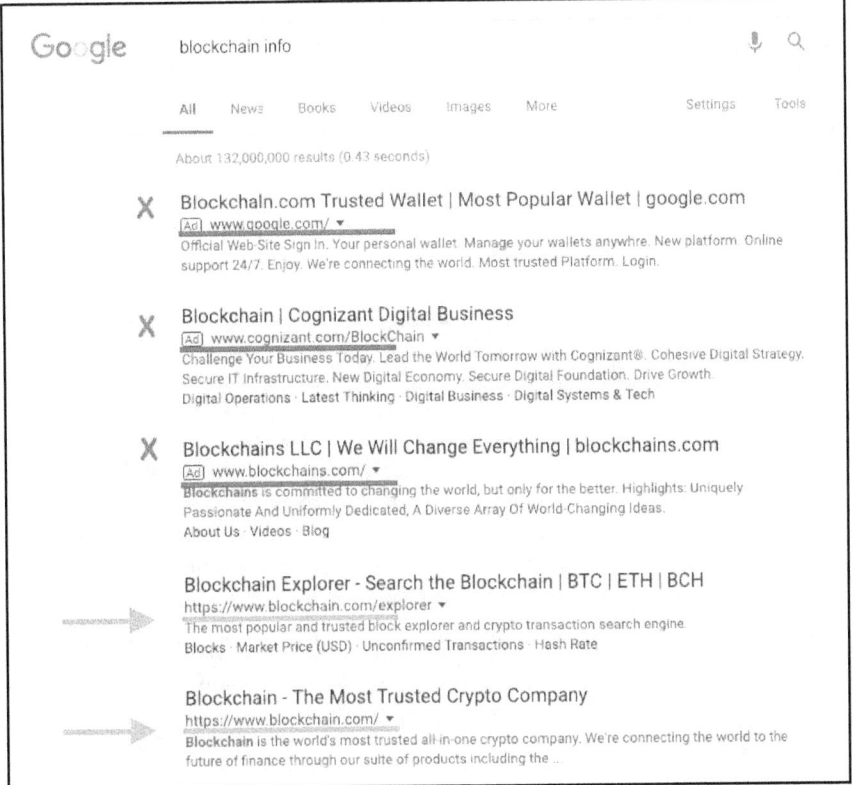

Although it is easier, it is extremely risky to click on the first result on Google Search for cryptocurrency-related terms. Bitcoin websites that you use frequently such as your exchange or wallet websites should be verified and bookmarked to make sure that you are at the correct website at all times.

Remember, there is no need for these websites to know your private keys for any reason whatsoever. As such, you should never disclose your private keys to anyone, even if you are prompted to do so.

Metal Storage Backup Tools

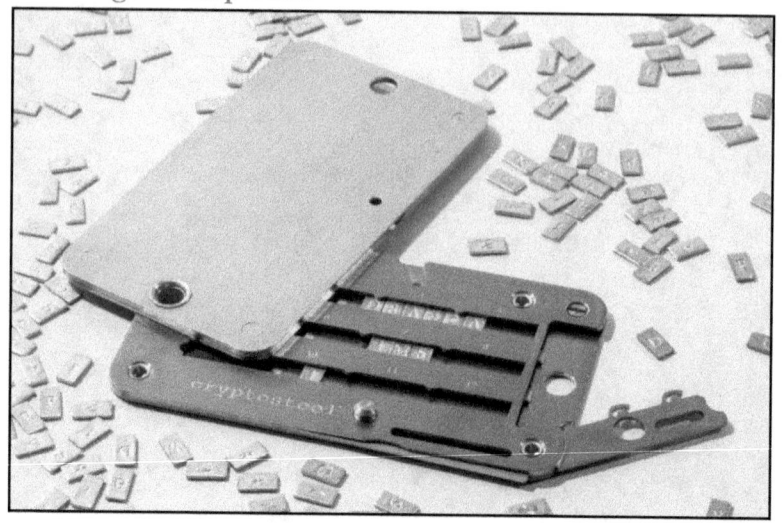

If you have some bitcoin stored in a non-custodial wallet, then chances are that you are the only person that has access to your private keys and seed phrase. As such, proper storage of the sensitive information is amongst the first steps needed in keeping your funds safe.

You may choose to write your seed phrase on a piece of paper and store it in a secure location, but this may not be ideal due to the natural wear and tear of the material.

To keep the seed phrase secure against natural elements, you may want to consider storing your seed phrases on a stainless steel metal tool that will protect against fire, water, insects, acid, and other natural elements.

Some popular companies that produce these metal devices include Cryptosteel, Cryptotag Zeus, and Cobo Tablet. Fashioned in the shape of capsules and cassettes, these products allow you to lock your seed phrase into a highly resistant shell that ensures maximum longevity.

Summary

Hackers are always on the lookout for potential targets to score an easy payday. As such, it is important to keep your Bitcoin wallets safe and secure. Hardware wallets such as Trezor or Ledger are highly recommended for bitcoin storage since your funds are stored offline. This significantly reduces the risk of getting attacked and should be the primary method for you to store most of your bitcoin.

It is also recommended that you backup the seed phrase used to generate the hardware wallet using a metal storage backup tool such as Cryptosteel. These products have been designed specifically to store your seed phrase in a more protective way.

Although we have recommended some wallets over others, it is not necessary to restrict yourself to using only one wallet. In fact, it may be better to use a few different wallets instead of putting all your funds in one wallet.

For example, you may choose to put the bulk of your funds which you don't intend to use on a day-to-day basis into a cold wallet like Trezor. Funds earmarked for active use, such as trading, may be placed in hot wallets such as your account at a centralized exchange.

Ultimately, choosing which bitcoin wallets to use depends on your own comfort level and preference. You should evaluate your use case and consider the pros and cons of each type of wallet to make the best possible decision.

CHAPTER 5: GETTING YOUR FIRST BITCOIN

Now that you know the basics behind how Bitcoin works, it's time to learn how to get your first bitcoin and how to store them safely. There are three broad ways to get bitcoin: buying, earning and mining. We will look into each of these methods in deeper detail in this chapter.

Buying Bitcoins

The easiest way to get your first bitcoin is to buy it directly. You could buy it from a friend, or from a cryptocurrency brokerage, exchange or peer-to-peer (P2P) marketplace.

Cryptocurrency brokerages, exchanges and P2P marketplaces are websites that allow you to buy or sell bitcoin. You can think of them as online money changers which facilitate the conversion of fiat currencies such as US Dollars into bitcoin and vice versa.

Cryptocurrency brokerages make it simple to buy or sell bitcoin as it abstracts away the orderbook concept and shows just the current buy and sell price. The simplicity that cryptocurrency brokerages offer comes at a cost of higher transaction fee compared to cryptocurrency exchanges. The most popular cryptocurrency brokerage is Coinbase.

Cryptocurrency exchanges, on the other hand, are cheaper but more complex. Users will need to interact with an orderbook to make buy or sell orders, a process which can be daunting for most beginners. Some popular exchanges that cater to sophisticated investors are Coinbase Pro, Kraken, Gemini, and Bitstamp.

Orderbook

An orderbook is an electronic list of buy and sell orders. It lists the number of units available for sale (ask) or requested to be purchased (bid) at each price point. An orderbook aggregates all the buy and sell orders currently available on the exchange.

You can buy or sell at the best price currently available (market order) or set a price you are willing to buy or sell (limit order). When you make a market order, you are known as the maker while if you buy at the best price currently available, you are known as the taker. Exchanges usually charge a lower fee for makers compared to takers.

P2P marketplaces operate more similarly to eBay—users are free to post the price they are willing to buy or sell bitcoin. Unlike cryptocurrency exchanges which aggregate all the buy and sell orders in an orderbook, P2P marketplaces do not aggregate these orders and you will have to choose the person you would like to trade with. The reputation system on P2P marketplaces is extremely important as the reliability of the seller in delivering the bitcoin or fiat currencies once the trade is done is a key consideration. Some examples of P2P marketplaces are LocalBitcoins, Remitano, and Paxful.

Generally speaking, buying your first bitcoins from a regulated cryptocurrency exchange is recommended over other options. Its regulated nature means that it has gone through strict due diligence by the financial regulators with stringent processes in place. Additionally, the customer support is usually better and if anything goes wrong, you can always report them to regulatory bodies.

Cryptocurrency Brokerages

This section will show you how to buy your first bitcoin from Coinbase. The platform allows bitcoin purchase via bank transfers and credit cards, with fees ranging between 1.49%-3.99%.

Buying bitcoin requires you to go through a Know-Your-Customer (KYC) process, where you are required to verify your identity by submitting various personal information such as your legal name, address, driving license or passport, and utility statement. The verification process may take a few days, but once you are verified, you are free to purchase bitcoins using your local fiat currency.

Cryptocurrency brokerages are not as widely available compared to cryptocurrency exchanges. We will explain further in the next section.

Coinbase

Step 1: Register for a Coinbase account.

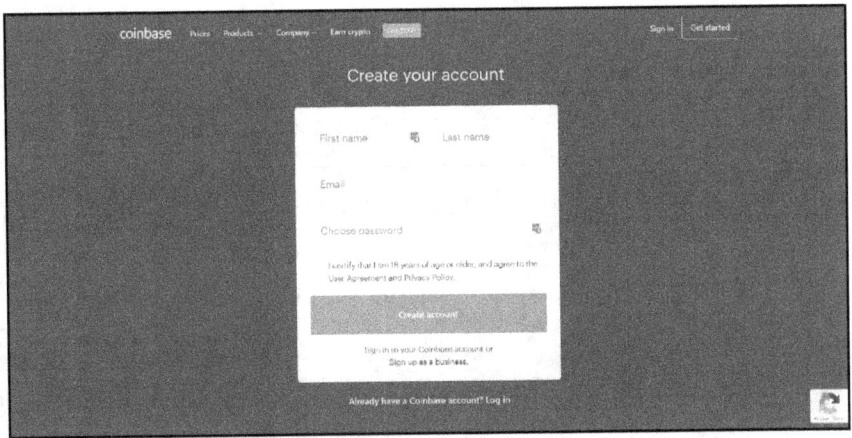

Step 2: Verify your email address.

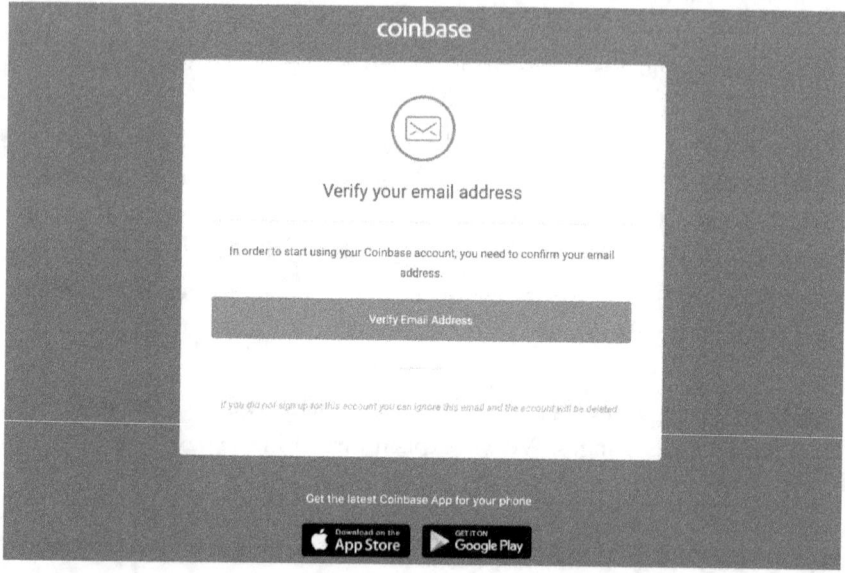

Step 3: Set up two-step verification using your mobile phone.

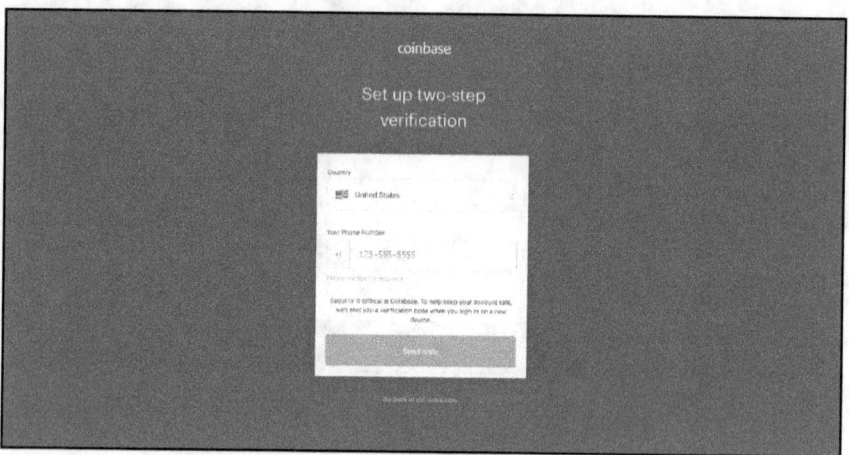

Step 4: Verify your identity (ID documents required).

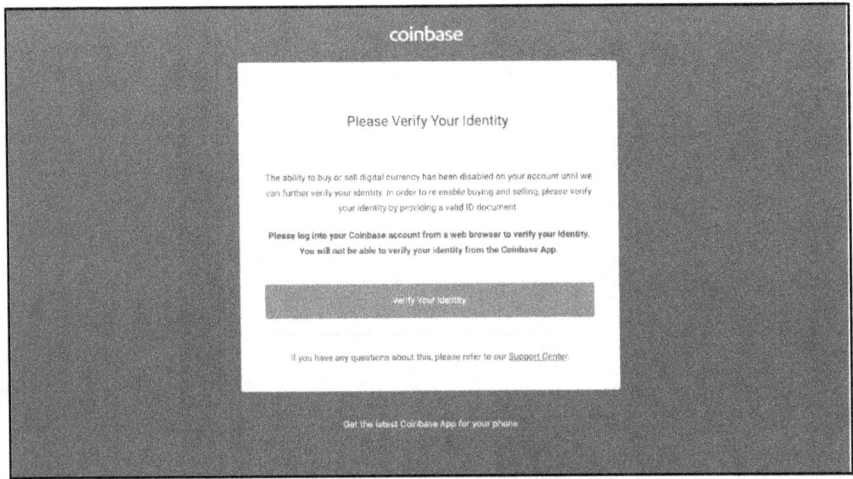

Step 5: Click on your profile picture in the top right corner and head to 'Settings' to enable two-factor authentication.

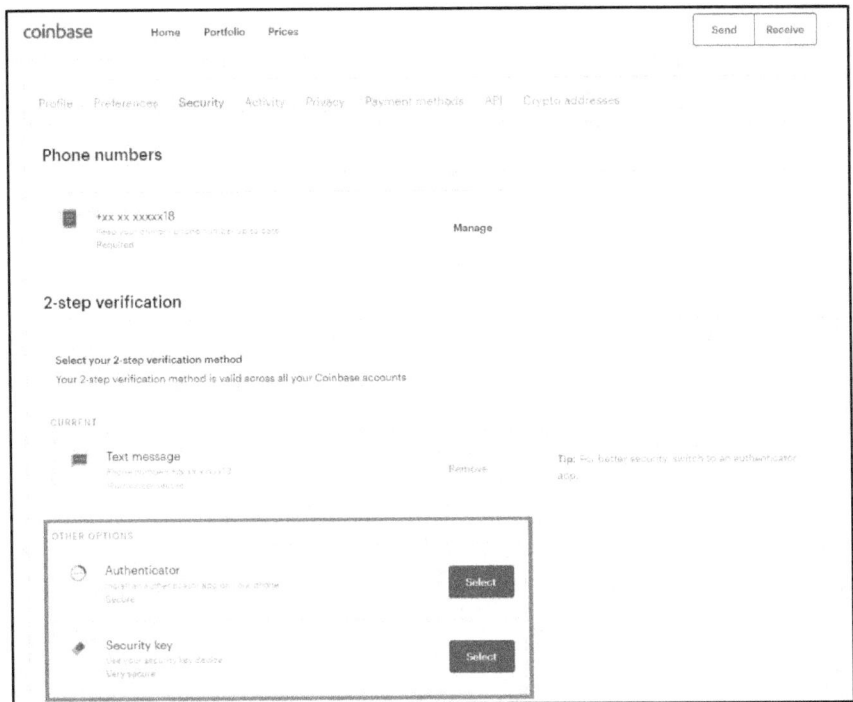

Step 6: Add a payment method to your account.

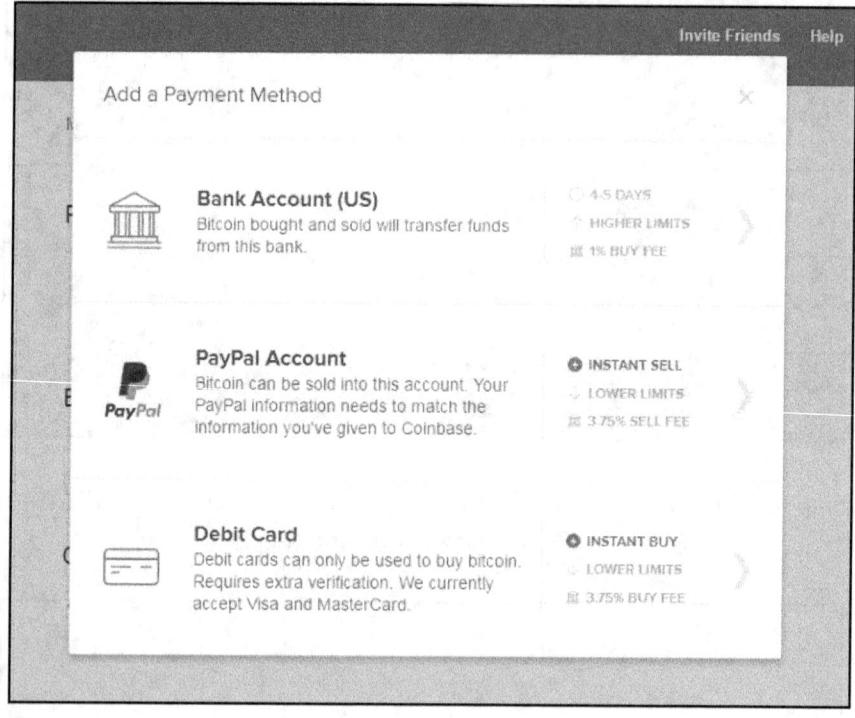

Step 7: Click on 'Trade' in the top-right corner of the dashboard and choose the cryptocurrency you would like to purchase.

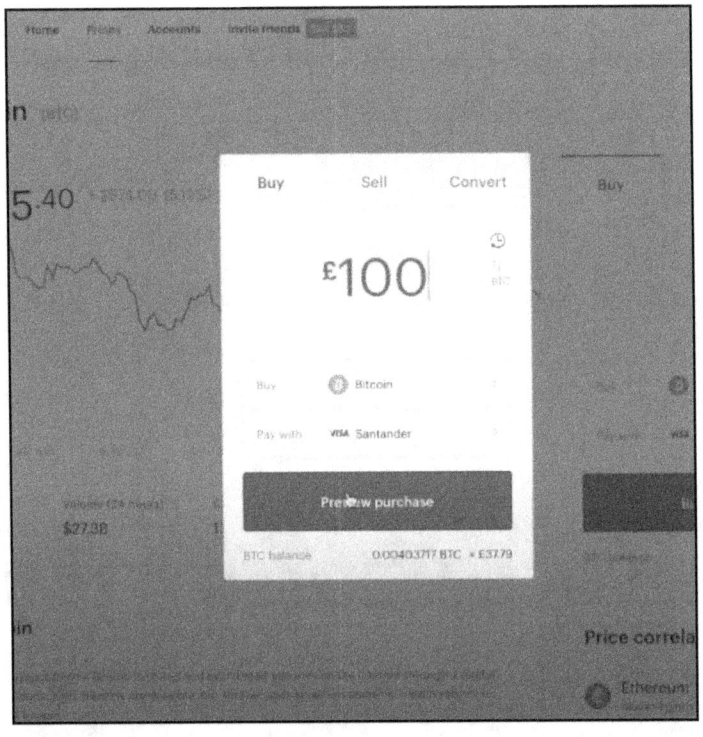

Step 8: Confirm the purchasing details and click on 'Buy Now' to complete your purchase.

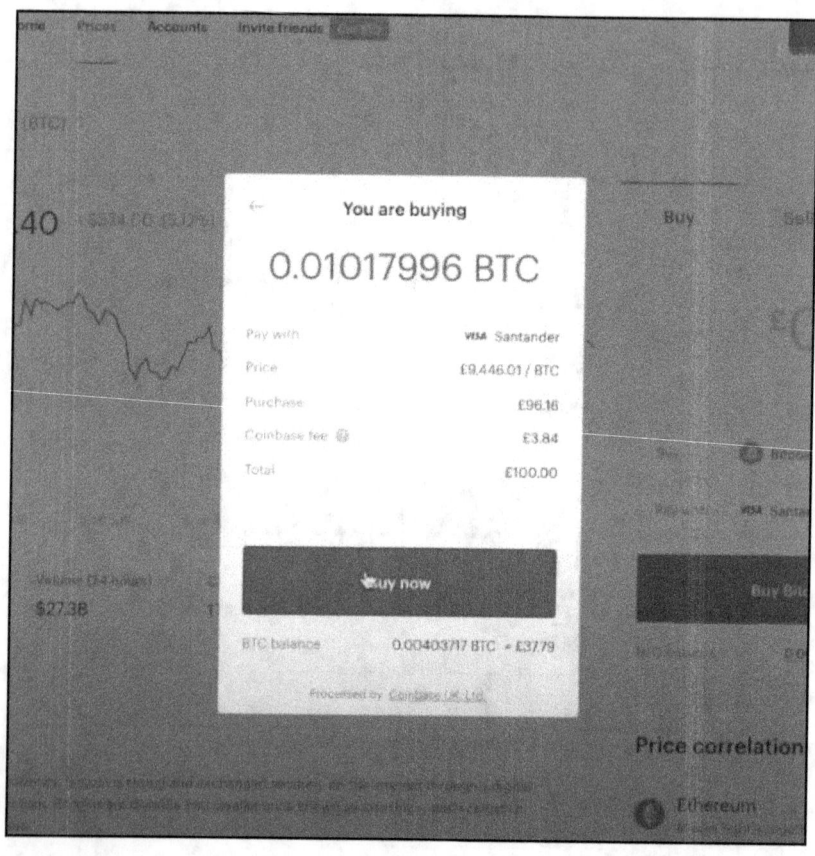

Cryptocurrency Exchanges

Many cryptocurrency exchanges are available in most countries, which each exchange supporting different fiat currencies. Depending on the jurisdiction, some cryptocurrency exchanges are regulated and some are not. You will need to do your own research by checking regulatory resources and assessing your risk tolerance level before proceeding with a cryptocurrency exchange.

Similar to cryptocurrency brokerages, you will need to go through the KYC process before you can purchase your first bitcoin on an exchange. A few notable platforms include Coinbase Pro, Kraken, and Gemini.

Let's walk through the process of buying bitcoin from Kraken.

Kraken

Kraken is one of the largest cryptocurrency exchanges in the world, serving over 170 countries and supporting more than 40 different coins and tokens. In 2020, Kraken became the first crypto exchange to obtain a bank license in the United States.[66]

Kraken has extensive trading pairs for each of their supported fiat currencies and hosts different types of accounts, so that you can choose the

---

[66] (2020, September 16). Kraken Becomes First Crypto Exchange to Become a US Bank ....
Retrieved November 23, 2020, from https://www.nasdaq.com/articles/kraken-becomes-first-crypto-exchange-to-become-a-us-bank-2020-09-16

one that best suits your needs. Here, we will show you the steps needed to buy bitcoins on Kraken.

Step 1: Go to www.kraken.com and click on Create Account button.

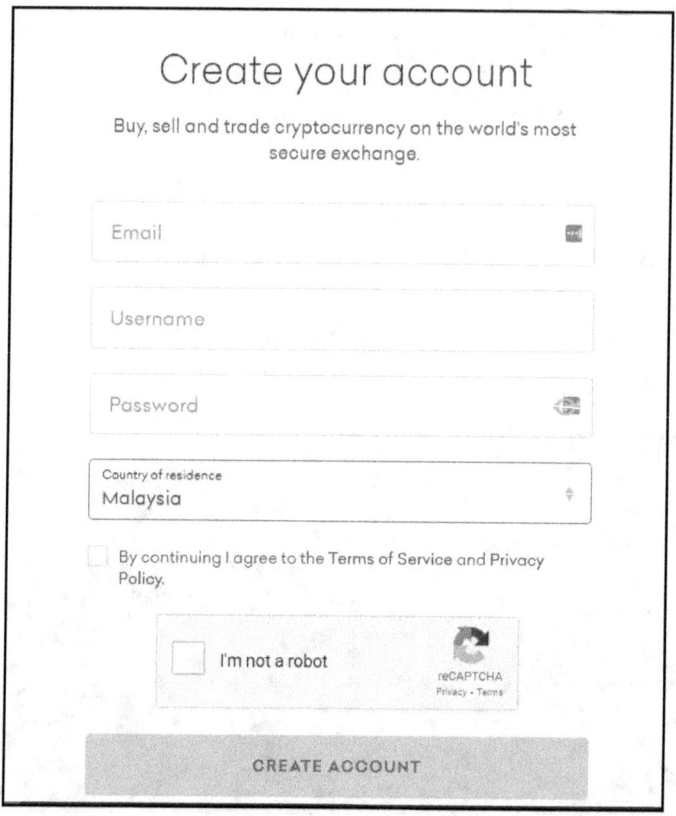

Step 2: Activate your account with the code emailed to you.

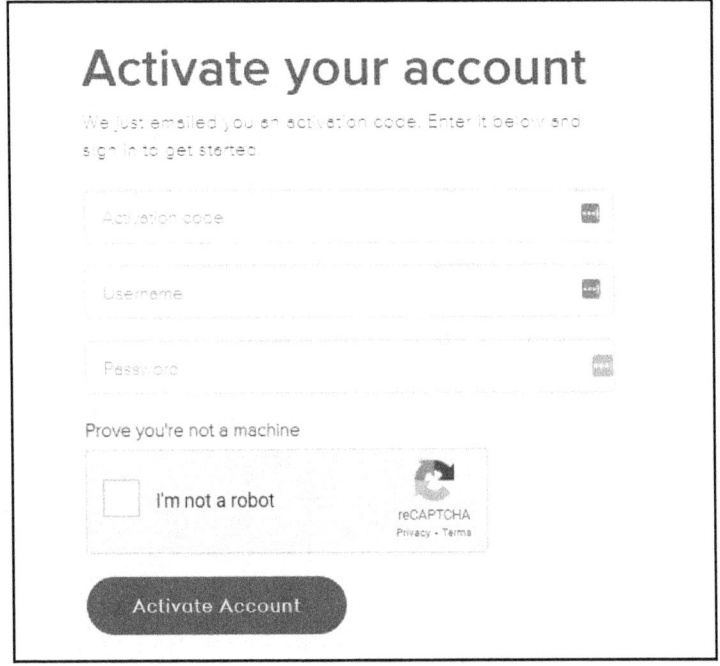

Step 3: To buy Bitcoin with fiat, you will need to select the Intermediate account and verify your identity by uploading a government-issued ID and proof of residence. It may take up to 24 hours for your account to be verified.

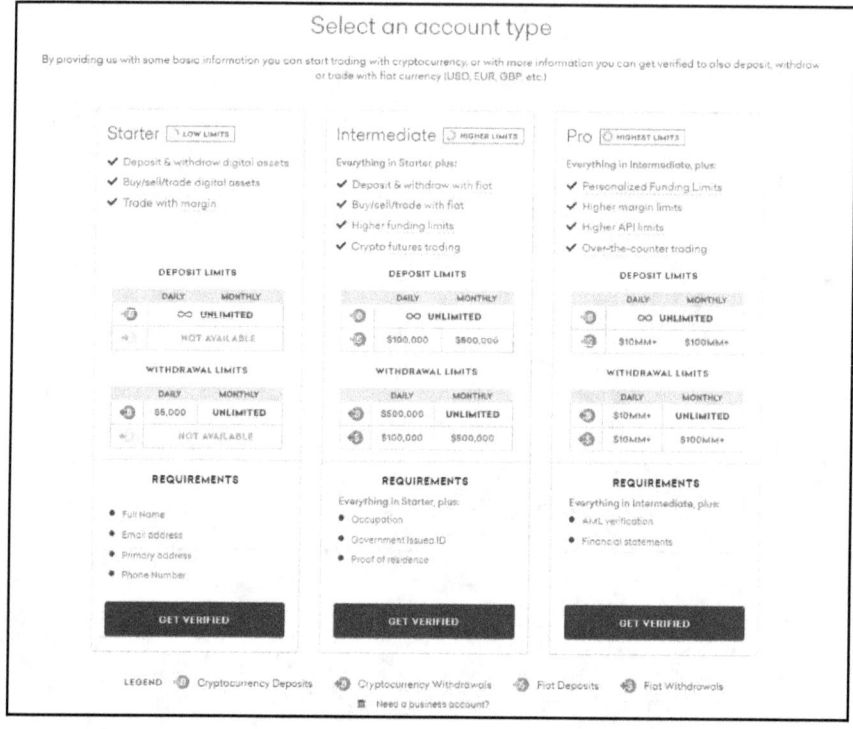

Step 4: Next, set up Two-Factor Authentication (2FA) to secure your Kraken account.

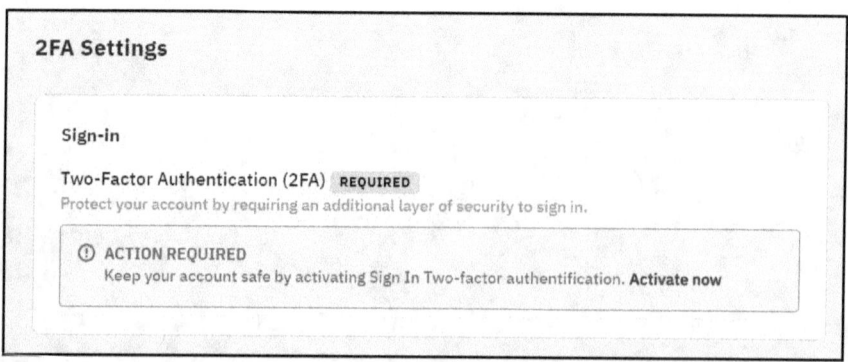

Step 5: Once you have set up your Two-Factor Authentication, you are all set to buy bitcoin. Click on the "Buy Crypto" button to move on with the next step.

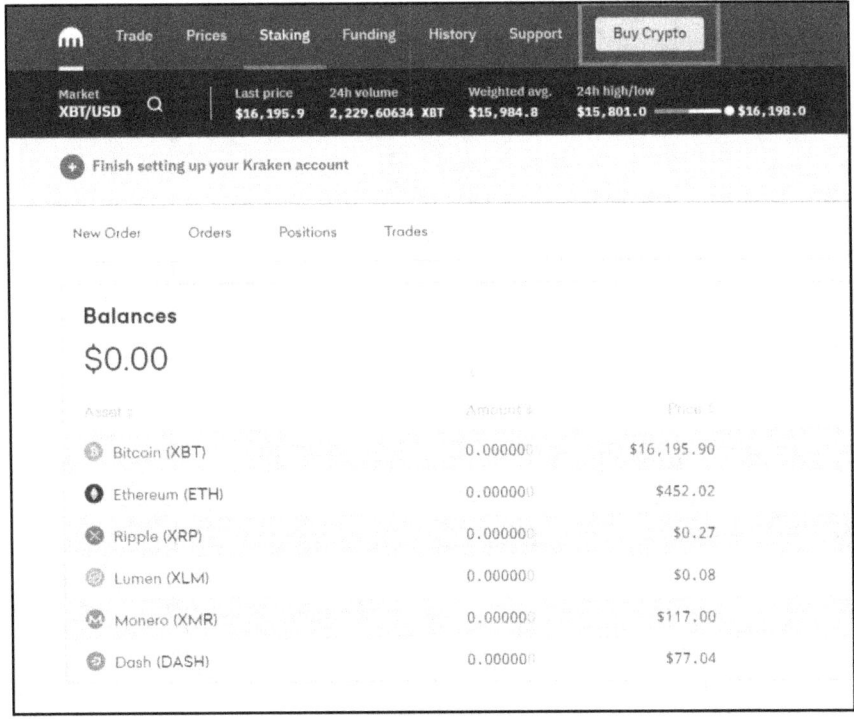

Step 6:   To buy bitcoin with fiat currencies, such as the US dollar, you must first deposit some funds into your account.

Peer-to-Peer (P2P) Marketplaces

If you live in a country without a feasible cryptocurrency exchange, you might consider using a peer-to-peer (P2P) marketplace. Similar to brokerages and exchanges, P2P marketplaces will also usually require you to go through a KYC process.

However, instead of buying bitcoin directly via cryptocurrency exchanges, P2P marketplaces connect buyers and sellers of bitcoin directly to each other. This means that you can choose which buyer or seller you would like to trade with.

Some well-known P2P marketplaces are LocalBitcoins, Binance P2P, Paxful, Remitano, and Hodl Hodl.

LocalBitcoins

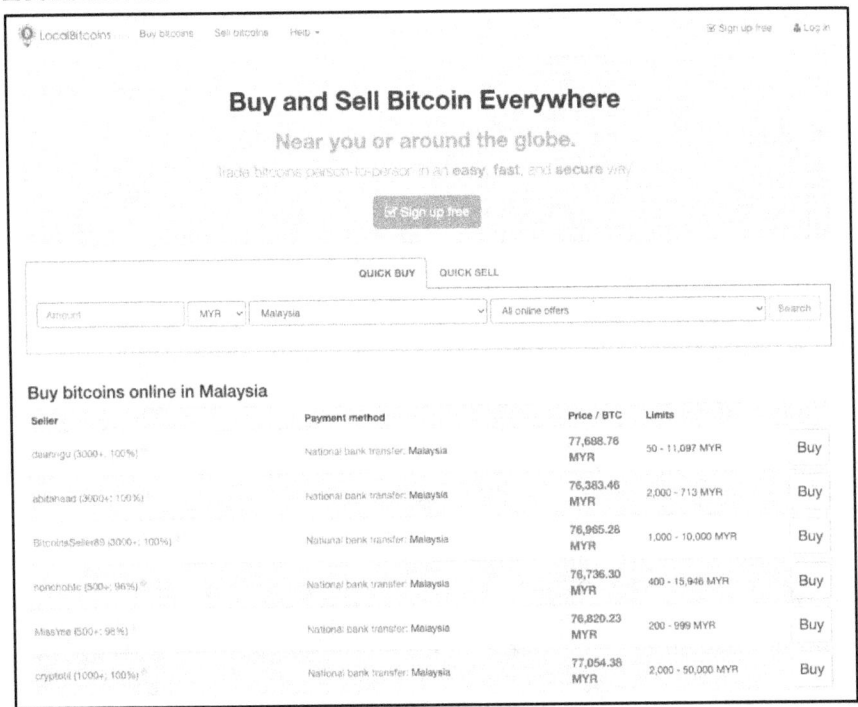

Founded in Finland in June 2012, LocalBitcoins is one of the largest P2P marketplaces in the world. It has facilitated bitcoin transactions between buyers and sellers in over 248 countries and 16,000 cities.[67]

Its simple user interface and support for many payment options have helped it garner a reputation for being accessible and easy to use. Let's walk through the steps to get started with buying your first bitcoin on LocalBitcoins.

---

[67] (n.d.). LocalBitcoins Review: Is LocalBitcoins Safe ... – CoinSutra. Retrieved November 10, 2020, from https://coinsutra.com/localbitcoins-review/

Step 1: Register your account by filling in your username, email and password.

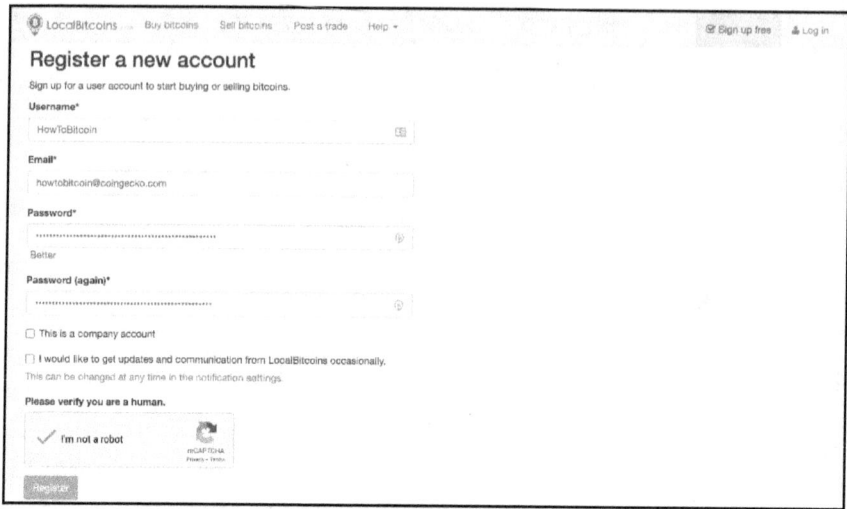

Step 2: Read through the Terms of Service and Privacy Policy. Scroll down and click "I Agree".

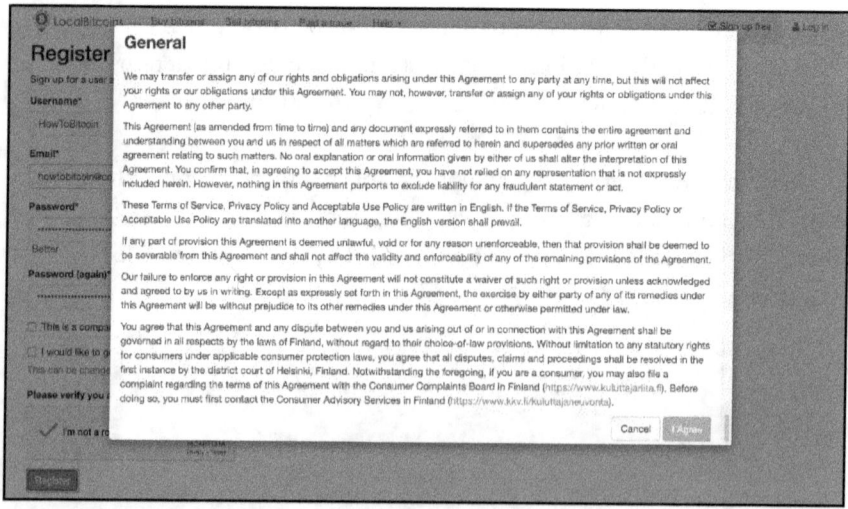

Step 3:   Check your email and click on the confirmation link.

Step 4:   Next, fill out your first name, last name and mobile phone number. They are needed for KYC and mobile verification processes in later steps.

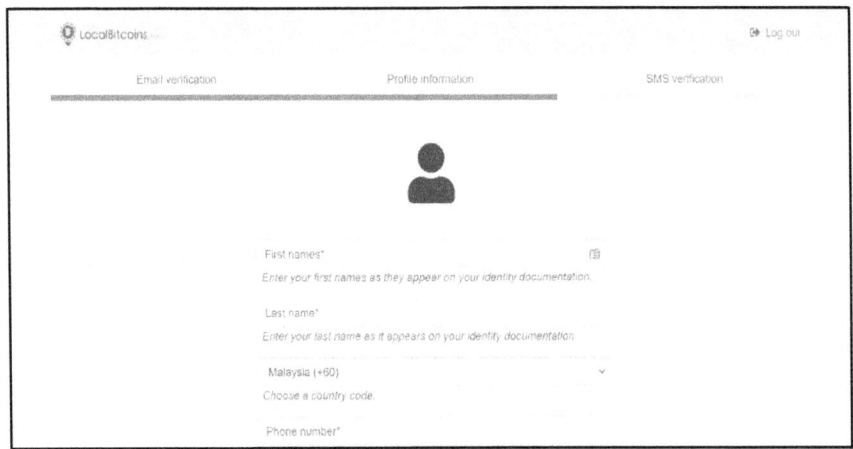

Step 5: A verification code will be sent via SMS to your mobile number. Input the code and click 'Submit'.

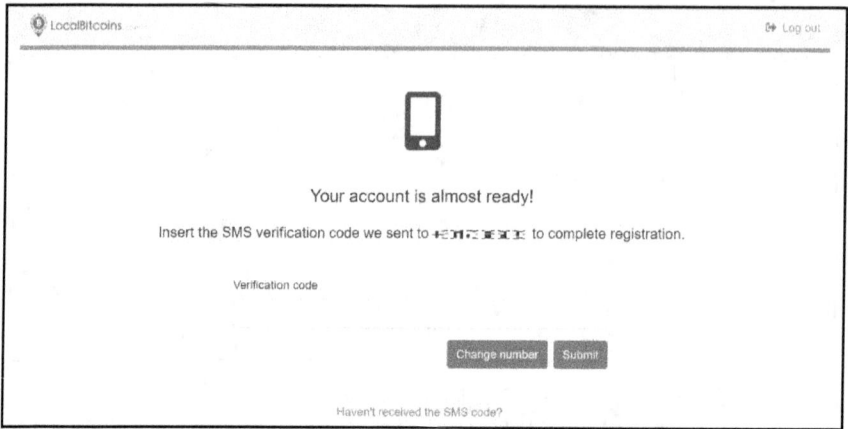

Step 6: You will be redirected to the trading dashboard. Before buying your first bitcoin, you will need to complete the KYC verification. Go to 'Profile' followed by 'Settings' and then 'Verification'.

In the box below, you will notice that you're at Tier 0. Most sellers require at least a Tier 1 verification level. Click 'Proceed to the next level' and follow the on-screen instructions.

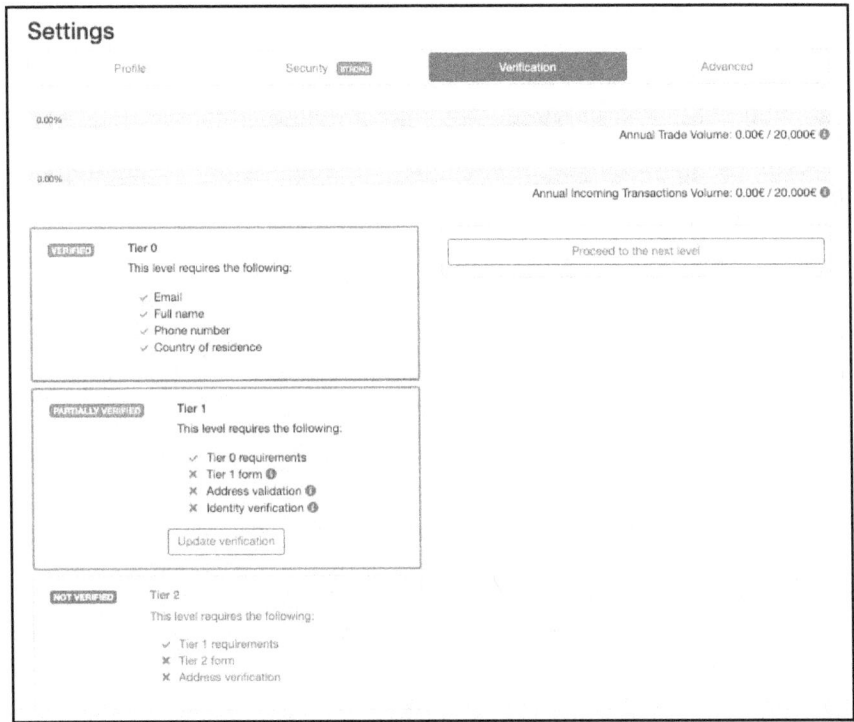

Step 7: After submitting your address and identity verification, you will be upgraded to Tier 1. With this upgrade, you can now buy your first bitcoin!

Return to the trading dashboard. Here, you can browse through the advertisements of numerous bitcoin sellers. Input the amount you are willing to spend, country and payment method to filter your options. Once you have chosen an ad, click 'Buy'.

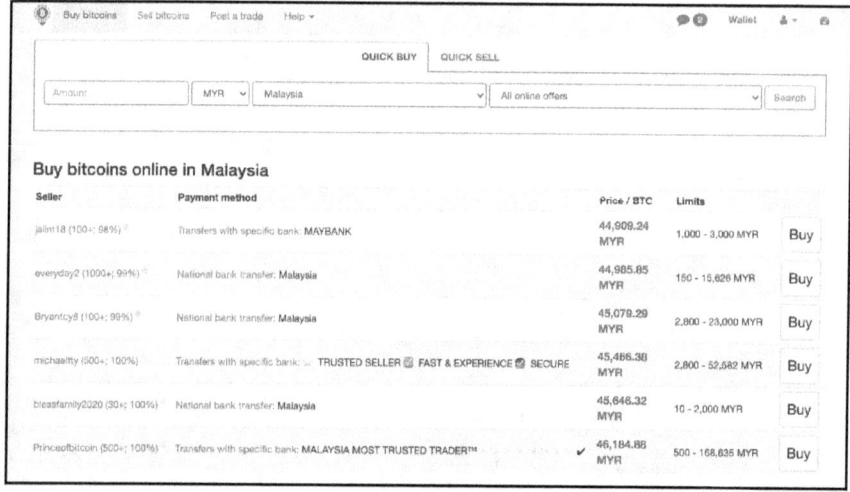

Protip: Look for sellers with a good reputation. You can identify them by looking at the number and coloured dot next to their name. Traders with better reputation will have a higher number and a green dot next to their names.

Step 8:   After clicking 'Buy', you will be redirected to the payment page. Input the amount you're willing to spend and carefully read the Terms of Trade specified by the seller. If everything looks agreeable, click 'Send trade request'.

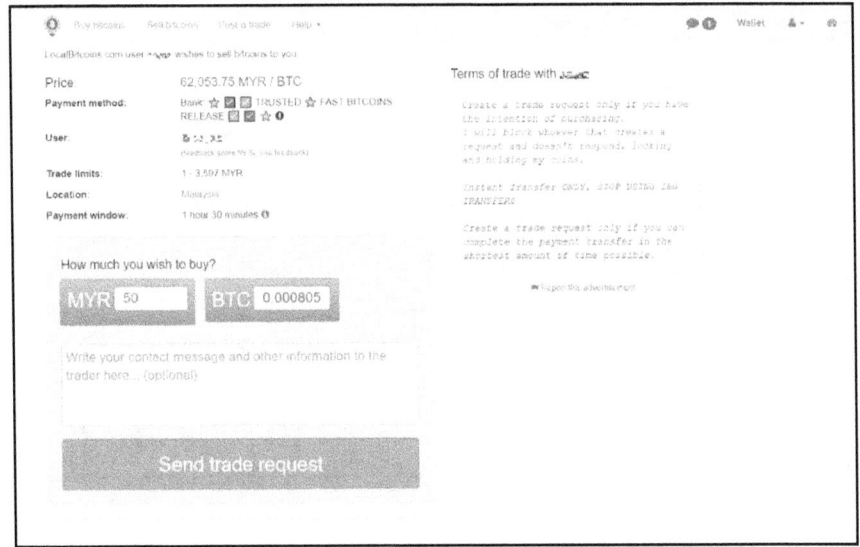

Step 9:   You will be requested to make your payment. Follow the on-screen instructions and complete the transaction within the payment window. Once done, click 'I have paid' and you should receive your bitcoin soon!

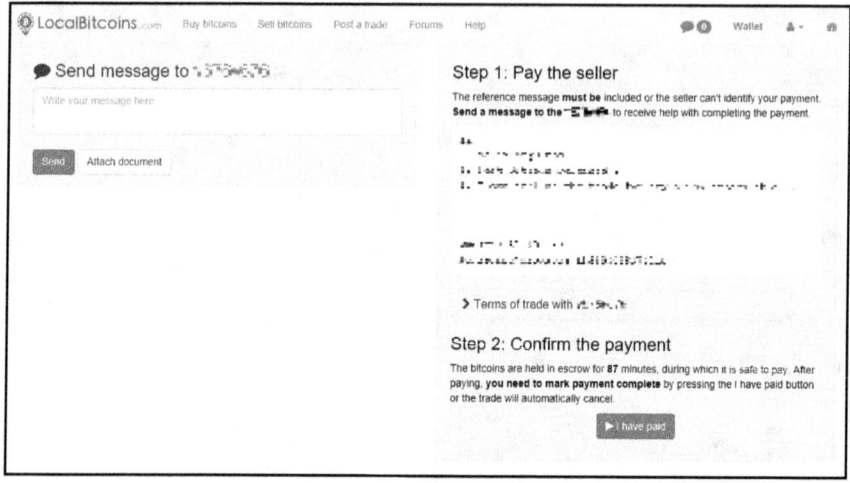

Step 10: To keep your bitcoin safe, you should transfer it to a wallet that you control. Click 'Wallet' on your dashboard and then 'Send bitcoins'. Copy and paste your wallet's address in the 'Receiving bitcoin address' field and set the amount you wish to transfer in BTC. After that, you are all set!

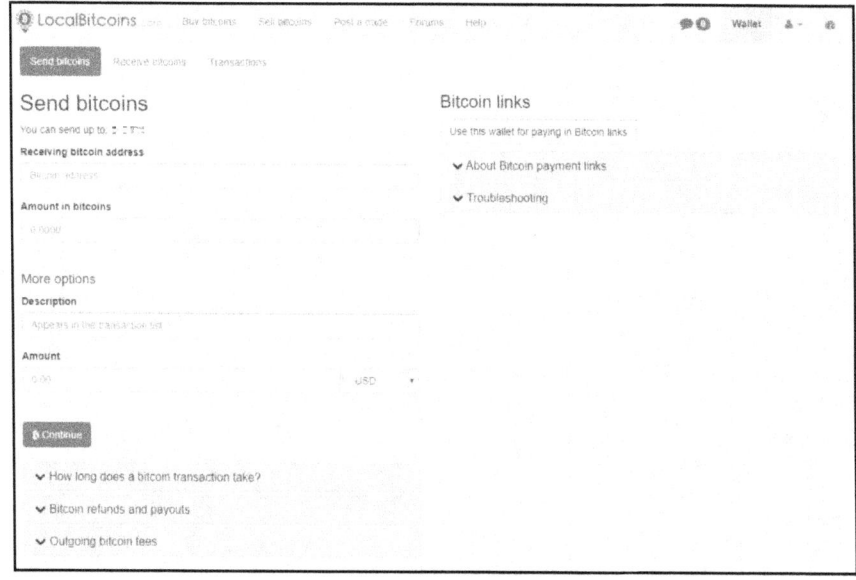

Earning Bitcoin

Bitcoin is money. Similar to money, you can earn bitcoin through various means.

While the most straightforward way to earn bitcoin is to ask your employer to pay a part (or all) of your salary in bitcoin, other alternative methods allow you to earn your bitcoin on the side.

Earn bitcoin cashback using Lolli

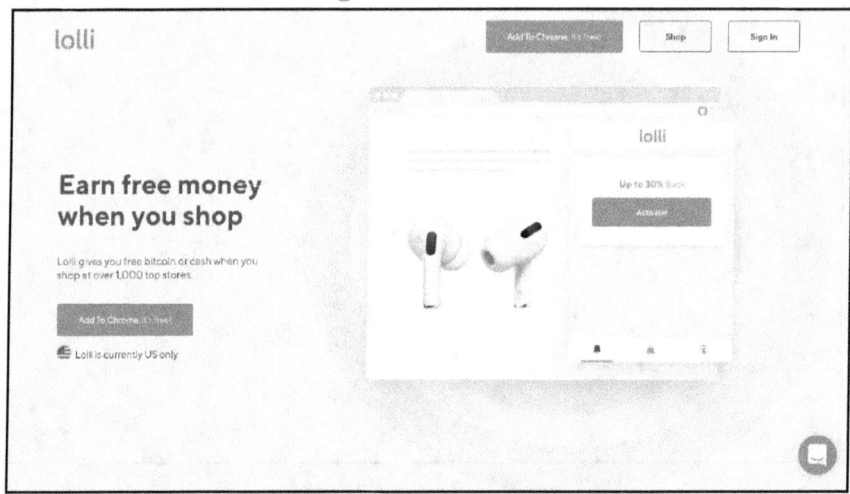

The Lolli bitcoin cashback program is identical to other cashback programs currently available. The way cashback programs work is that the cashback companies will share a percentage of the affiliate fees earned from purchases made from online retailers.

Most cashback companies pay in fiat currencies and directly to your bank account. In Lolli's case, your rewards are paid in bitcoin instead.

Lolli partners with many popular brands such as Nike, Sephora, Microsoft and Expedia. By using Lolli, you can start earning bitcoin while you go about your daily online purchases. Lolli pays anywhere from 1% up to 27% of cashback from the hundreds of merchants on their site. This is one of the easiest ways to earn bitcoin.

Do note that Lolli is currently only available in the United States.

Here's a step-by-step guide to get started with Lolli:

Step 1:   Register for a Lolli account at https://www.lolli.com/

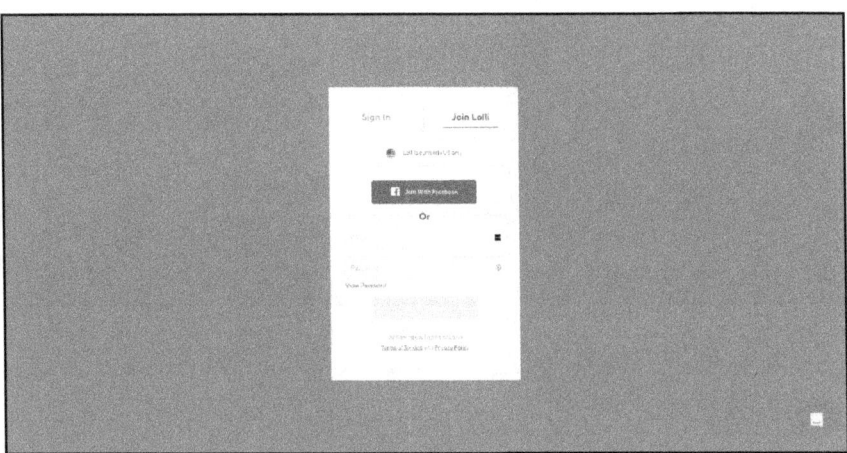

Step 2:   Once you have registered for an account, you can earn bitcoin as you shop by clicking the merchant's tracking links from the Lolli platform.

Step 3:   Do remember to claim your SatsTag.

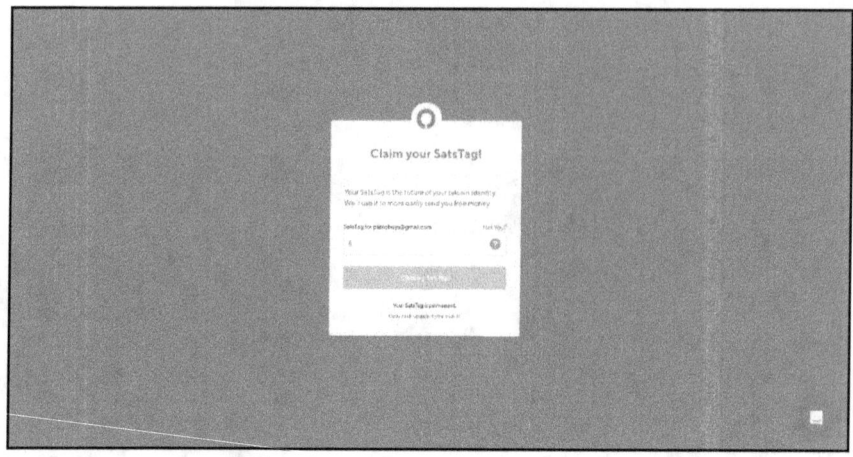

Step 4:   For an easier shopping experience, you can download the Chrome browser extension.

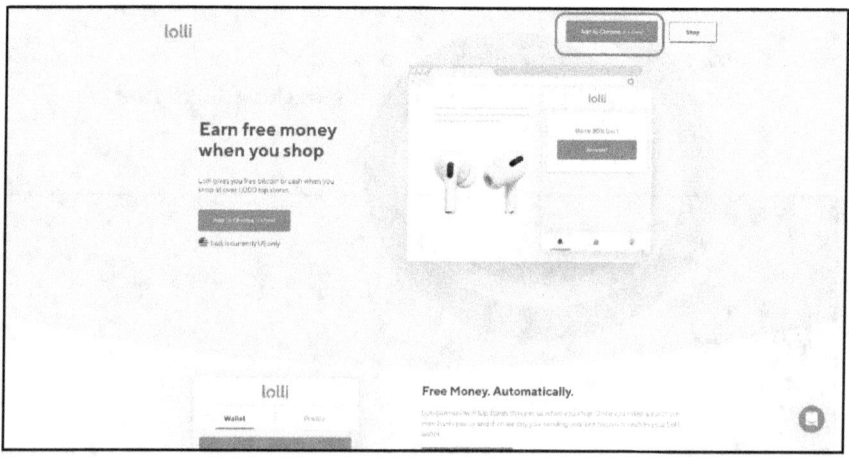

Provide services in exchange for bitcoin

If your employer does not want to pay you in bitcoin, you can trade your skills for bitcoin using crypto freelance platforms. Whether you are an accountant, website developer, social media manager, or copywriter, you can be compensated with bitcoin in exchange for the services that you provide.

Some of the more popular crypto freelance platforms include:

- Crypto.jobs – Website for blockchain jobs
- Cryptogrind – Dedicated bitcoin freelance platform
- Bitfortip – Website that tips you in bitcoin for being helpful
- MicroLancer – P2P task listing board where you can apply to published tasks and get paid in bitcoin using Lightning Network-supported wallets

Play to earn via bitcoin faucets

One of the more entertaining albeit slow way to earn free bitcoin is via bitcoin faucets. Bitcoin faucets give out tiny fractions of bitcoin every few hours for performing certain tasks, such as playing mobile or online games. These bitcoin faucets make money by showing ads to users and reward users for interacting with them. They are usually not worth your time, unless if you currently live in a developing country.

Disclaimer: CoinGecko is not affiliated with ANY of these games or products in any way. Please use at your own risk.

- Bitcoin Blast

  Bitcoin Blast by Bling Financial is a fun puzzle game available for Android users. You will be rewarded with Bling Points for every gameplay. With Bling Points, you can redeem bitcoin cashed out to your Coinbase wallet. The more you play, the more Bling Points that you will earn. Bling Financial also offers four other mobile games that reward users with Bling Points that can be converted into bitcoin.

- Bit Fun

Since its inception in 2017, Bit Fun is a classic bitcoin faucet website that allows users to claim bitcoin every few minutes. There are browser games available to play on their website whilst you wait for the next claiming cycle. Besides the games, users can also earn extra bitcoin by completing surveys and other offers available on their website.

Mining Bitcoin

All bitcoins were originally created through a process known as mining. In the early 2010s, mining was feasible for anyone with a computer as it can be done with a regular Central Processing Units (CPU).

As more people started mining bitcoin, the difficulty rate increased. Eventually miners needed more specialized machines to mine bitcoins. Some researchers found that Graphics Processing Units (GPU) and soon Field-Programmable Gate Array (FGPA) can be used to mine bitcoin more efficiently.

Eventually, this was quickly replaced by the more efficient machines known as Application Specific Integrated Circuit (ASIC). An ASIC miner is a device designed for a specific type of work which is to solve the complex Bitcoin mining puzzle at breakneck speed.

These days, it is no longer possible to mine bitcoin using CPU, GPU, or FGPA—only the most efficient ASIC miners can be used to mine bitcoin. You also need scale to be able to mine profitably.

For most beginners, it is **not recommended** that you get your first bitcoin through mining as it is very capital intensive and involves a lot of work. You will need to spend a lot of capital upfront in acquiring the latest ASIC miners, getting it delivered to a mining facility, setting it up, paying for electricity, maintaining the miners and so on.

It may take roughly 12 to 15 months before you earn enough to pay back the upfront investment made to purchase the ASIC miner and your return is also highly volatile due to fluctuating bitcoin prices and difficulty level. ASIC miners also go obsolete fast as newer and more efficient machines are released.

Cloud Mining

As you go around your research, you might come across providers who claim that they can help you mine bitcoin via cloud mining. Cloud mining is a service that allows you to outsource the work needed to mine bitcoin. The cloud mining operators will lease the ASIC miners to you and do all the work to maintain these machines. All you need to do is pay a fixed monthly fee to purchase some cloud mining contracts. These contracts typically provide a fixed amount of hashes per second where you will get to keep the bitcoin that is mined.

Although the contracts offered may sound tempting, there are a lot of risks with cloud mining as it assumes bitcoin price and difficulty will stay constant. As we covered in earlier chapters, bitcoin difficulty will go up over time and it is very hard to predict its price.

In most cases, you can only turn a profit if the bitcoin price goes up and you are lucky enough to sell it at a high price. *Most cloud mining operators charge a high monthly fee and you will most likely not be able to turn a profit from your cloud mining ventures!*

Similar to gold mining, Bitcoin mining is also a highly complex process and it is not recommended if your objective is to have an initial exposure to bitcoin. It is usually more straightforward to buy bitcoin over an exchange as opposed to mining it. We at CoinGecko recommend that you skip mining until a later stage when you are more familiar with the pros and cons of Bitcoin mining.

CHAPTER 6: STORING YOUR BITCOIN SAFELY

After purchasing your first bitcoin on an exchange or a peer-to-peer marketplace, you should consider moving it to a non-custodial wallet that you control. In an earlier chapter, we explained the concept of bitcoin custody and why a non-custodial wallet may be a safer option for storing your bitcoin long-term.

We at CoinGecko recommend the use of hardware wallets to store your cryptocurrencies. There are several hardware wallet providers in the market. In this chapter, we provide step-by-step guides to help you set up some of the more popular non-custodial bitcoin wallets such as Trezor and Ledger.

Hardware Wallet: Trezor One

Purchasing a Trezor One hardware wallet will set you back around $100-200 depending on the model and location for delivery. Remember, always buy it from the manufacturer's websites directly as you do not want to take the risk of your devices being tampered with by a hacker from a non-reputable shop. Do not click on any Google Ads when navigating to the manufacturer's websites either because some of these ads could be scammers impersonating the real manufacturers' websites.

Let's go through the setting up of a Trezor One hardware wallet. It is currently retailing for $57 on the Trezor website[68].

Step 1: The Trezor Bridge is an application that is needed to facilitate communication between the Trezor wallet and the web browser.[69] To install it, head to https://wallet.trezor.io/#/bridge and download the latest version of Trezor Bridge. Simply select your operating system to get the latest version.

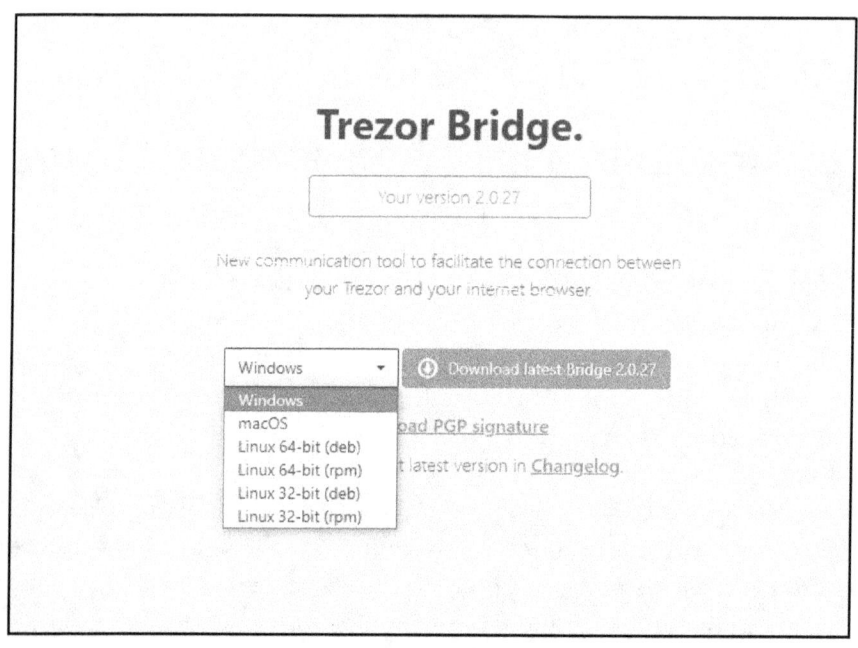

---

[68] (n.d.). Official Trezor Shop | Trezor Black – Trezor Model T. Retrieved November 16, 2020, from https://shop.trezor.io/product/trezor-one-black

[69] (2020, June 22). Trezor Bridge – Trezor Wiki. Retrieved January 20, 2021, from https://wiki.trezor.io/Trezor_Bridge

Step 2: Choose a destination folder and tap on "Install". Once complete, you can start the setup of your Trezor wallet.

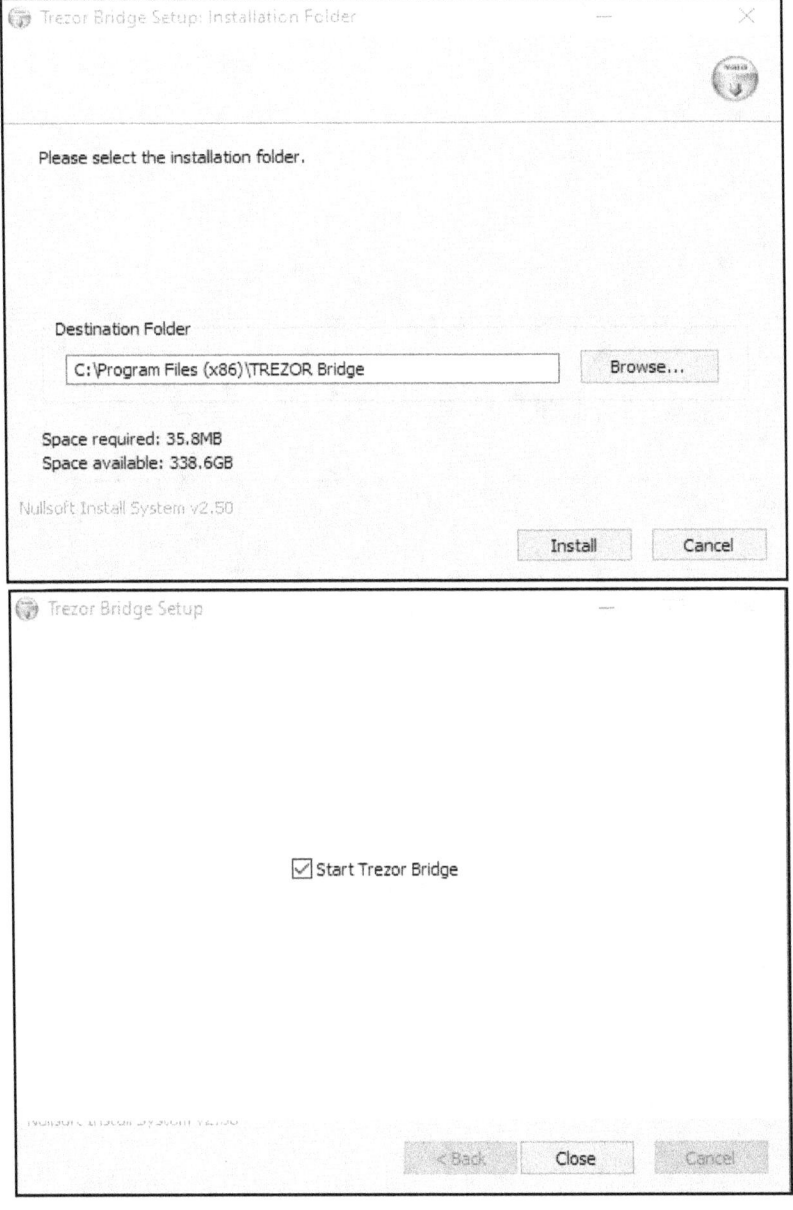

Step 3: Plug in your new Trezor to your computer and navigate to https://wallet.trezor.io/. Click on the "Create a wallet" button.

Step 4: Once you have created a new wallet, you will be requested to backup your wallet.

Step 5: On the next screen, you will see a warning for you to store your recovery seed safely. Do not take pictures of it nor store it on your computer. This is **important** because the data stored on your phone or computer may not be secure—hackers may get access to it, thus compromising your entire balance on Trezor. The best way to store your recovery seed is to use a metal device like Cryptosteel.

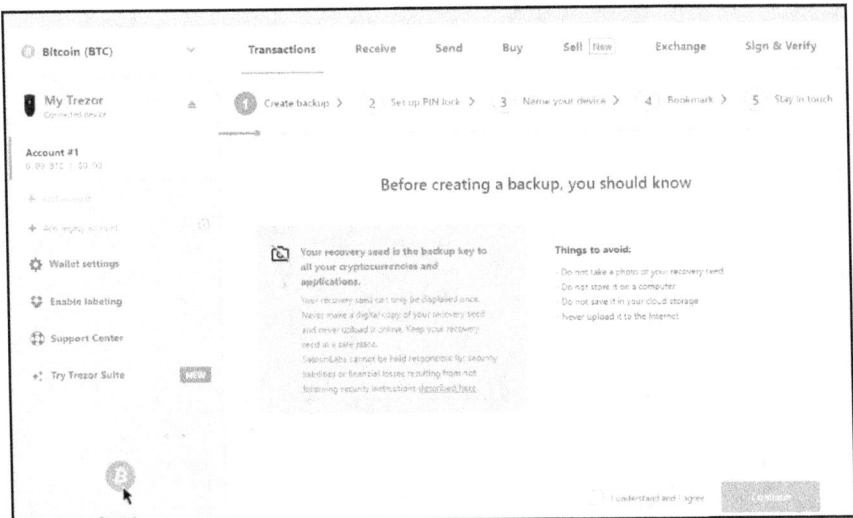

Step 6: Once you understand and agree, check the box and begin writing down your seed. Each word will appear on the screen of the Trezor, and after writing down each word, you will need to reconfirm. The recovery seed is 24 words-long.

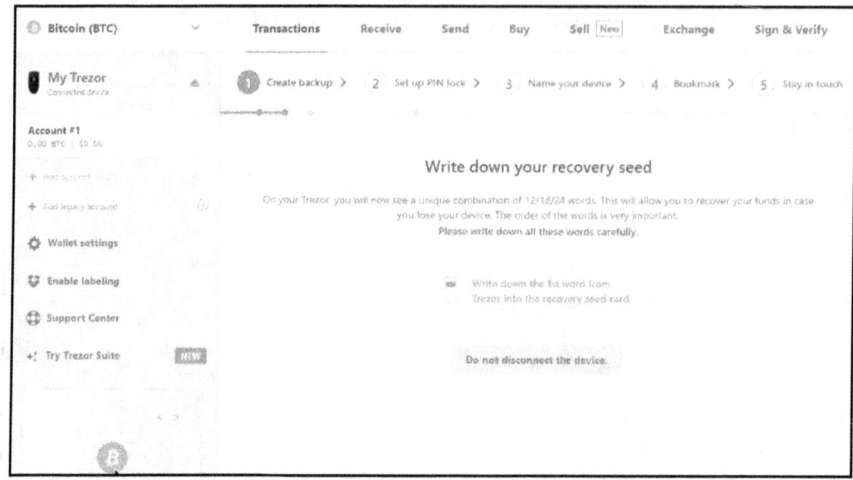

Step 7: After backing up your Trezor, set a strong PIN for your wallet. The numbers will appear on the hardware wallet in a random order. Select the numbers on the web interface.

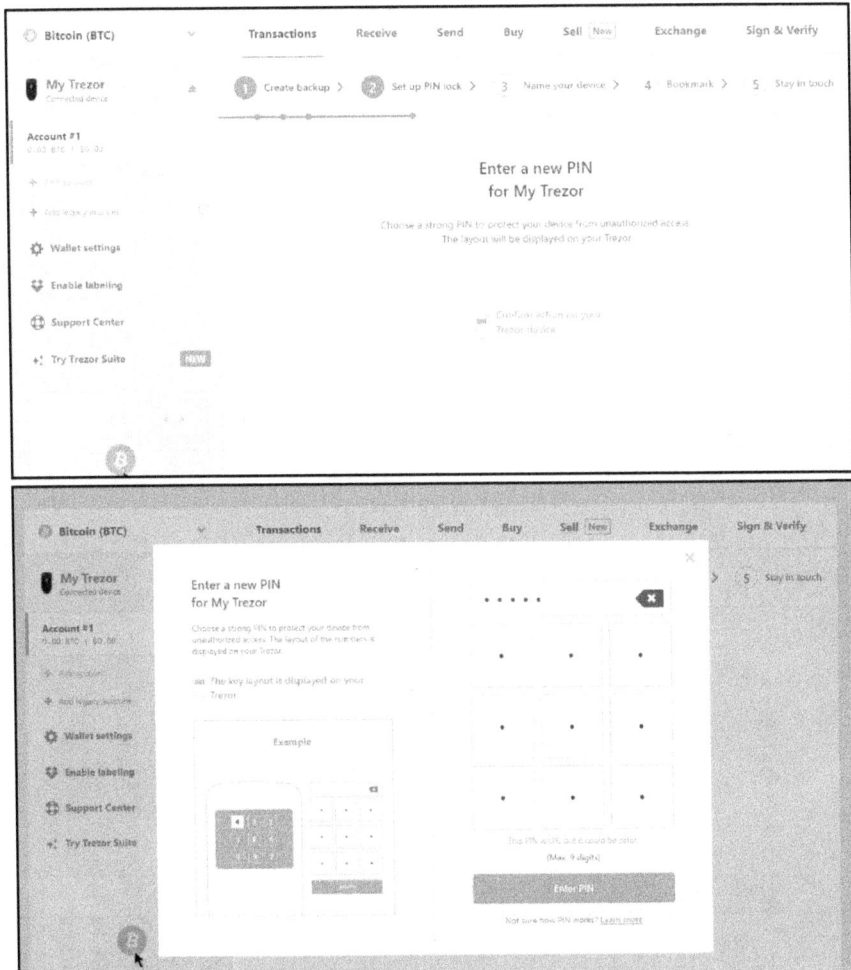

Step 8: Next, you will be prompted to name your wallet. We named ours "How To Bitcoin". You can change the name in the settings page.

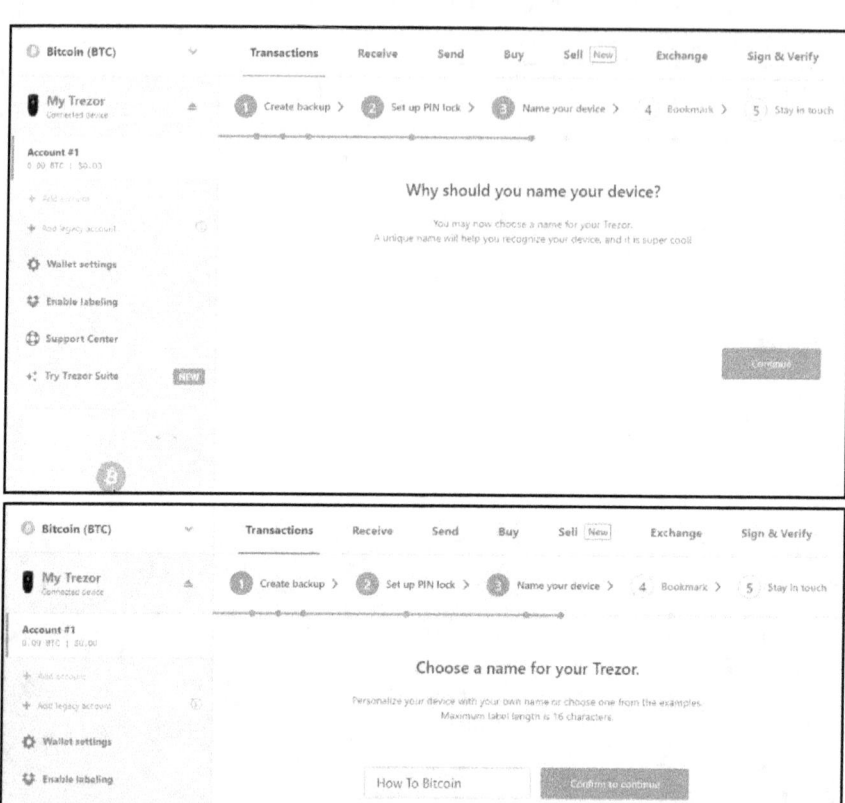

Step 9: When available, you may need to update the firmware version to the latest version. Simply disconnect your Trezor and then connect it back while holding both buttons down. Ensure that your recovery seed is backed up, and proceed with the update.

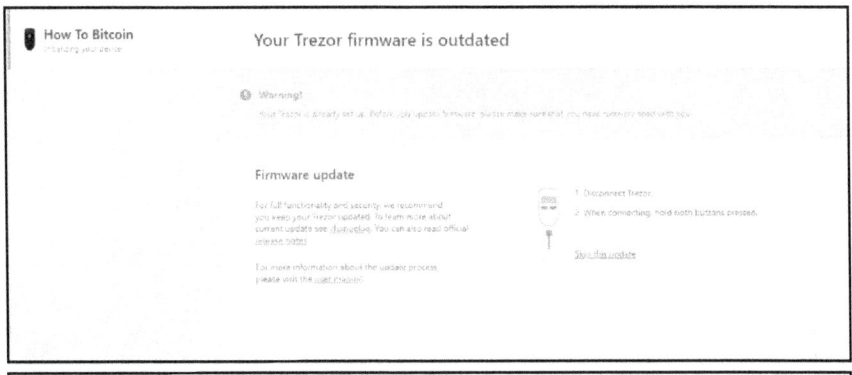

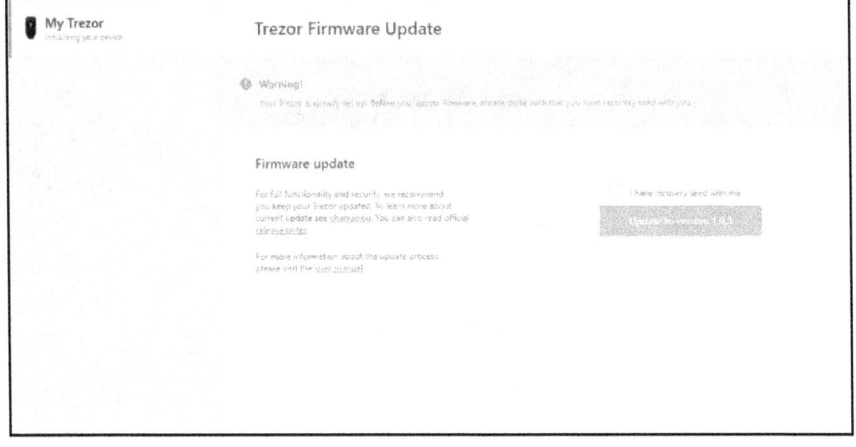

Step 10: Your Trezor is now ready! To receive bitcoin, simply tap on the "Receive" tab and select "Show full address." Cross-check the address and confirm it on the Trezor device. You can use this Bitcoin address to receive bitcoin.

Step 11: If you would like to send bitcoin instead, tap on the "Send" tab. Then, paste the address and key in the amount. The fee can be changed as well, with speeds ranging from Slow to Fast. The higher the fee, the faster the transaction will go through.

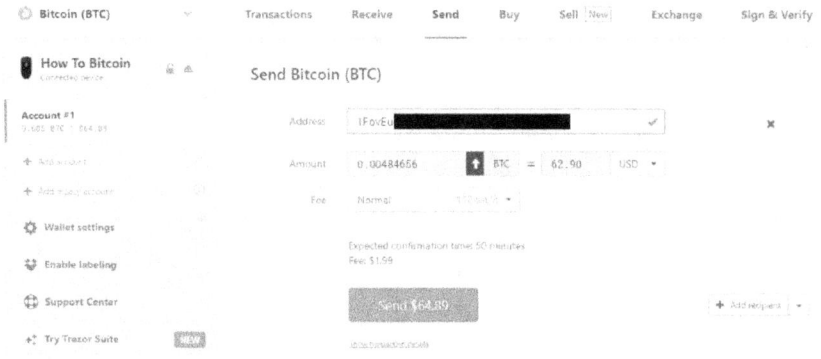

Step 12: Once done, hit the Send button and confirm it on your Trezor. You have just sent bitcoin on your Trezor! You can also Enable labeling on your Trezor to put notes on your transactions. It will connect with a cloud storage tool like Dropbox to store notes of your transactions.

Pro Tip: Adding a 25th word to your passphrase

Adding a 25th word can be thought of as a way to extend your recovery seed. This word can be chosen by you, and will further encrypt your recovery seed. If your 24 word recovery seed is compromised, the person holding those words will need the 25th word to access your funds.

However, it should be noted that adding a 25th word will generate an entirely different root key which will derive a different private key, public key, and address. If you forgot your 25th word, you will lose access to your funds.

Pro Tip 2: Shamir Backup

Shamir Backup allows you to split your seed into multiple shares.[70] In order to recover your wallet, you will need a certain number of these shares. The number of shares generated ranges between 1 and 16, which you can determine. Each share consists of a sequence of 20 or 33 words.

When recovering your wallet, there is a threshold that needs to be reached. This is the predetermined number of shares needed to recover a wallet. For example, if your Shamir Backup consists of 10 recovery shares, and you set the threshold to be "5 out of 10", you will need to key in any five of these 10 shares to recover your wallet.

Note: Shamir Backup is currently only available on Trezor Model T.

---

[70] (2020, January 22). Shamir Backup – Trezor Wiki. Retrieved January 20, 2021, from https://wiki.trezor.io/Shamir_Backup

Blockchain.com Mobile Wallet

Step 1: Head to Google Play or the Apple App Store to download the app.

Step 2: Create your wallet by filling in your email address and entering a strong password.

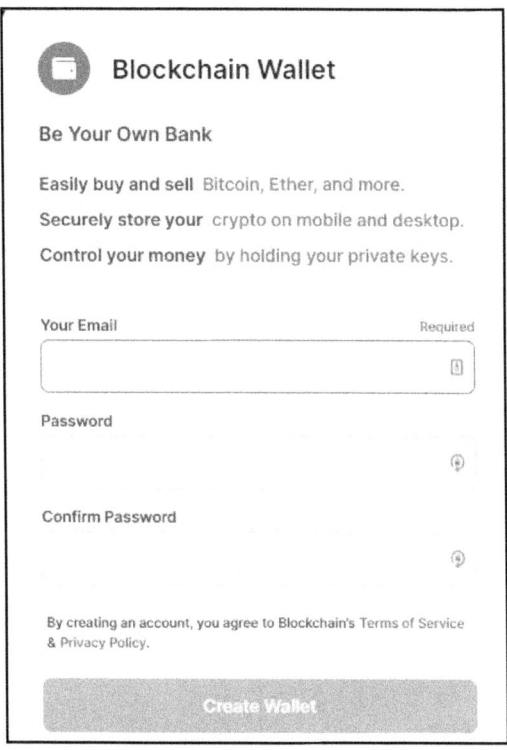

Step 3: Tap on the "Create Wallet" and follow the instructions on-screen. Once done, you will be greeted with a welcome message.

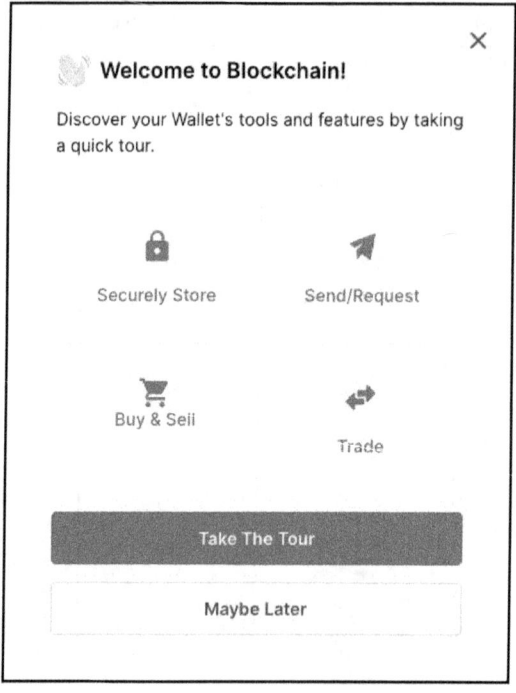

Step 4: After the welcome message, you will be transported to the dashboard. To transfer funds to your wallet, tap on 'Transfer'.

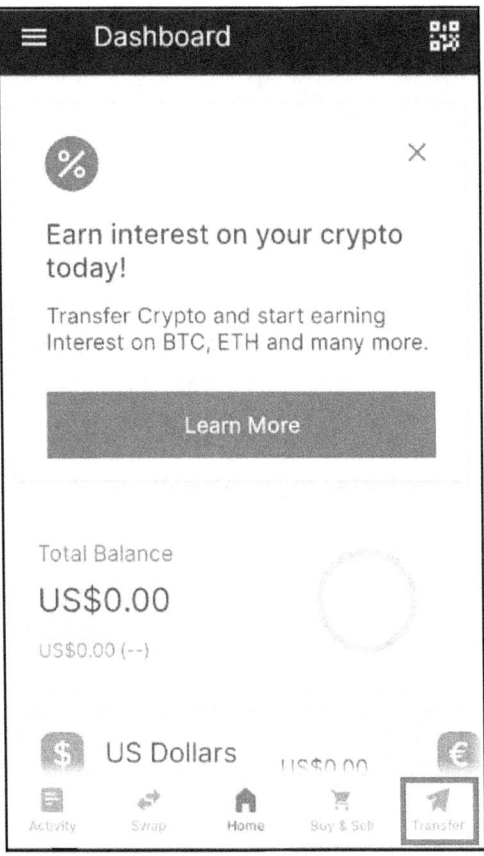

Step 5: On the 'Transfer' page, tap on 'Receive'. You will see a list of wallets for assets supported on Blockchain.com. Tap on Bitcoin.

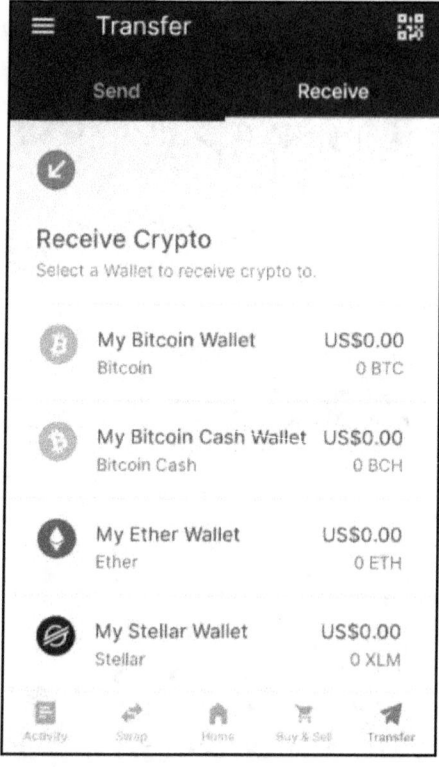

Step 6: Transfer your assets to the specified address or simply scan the QR Code. Be sure to double-check the address before you proceed to the next step.

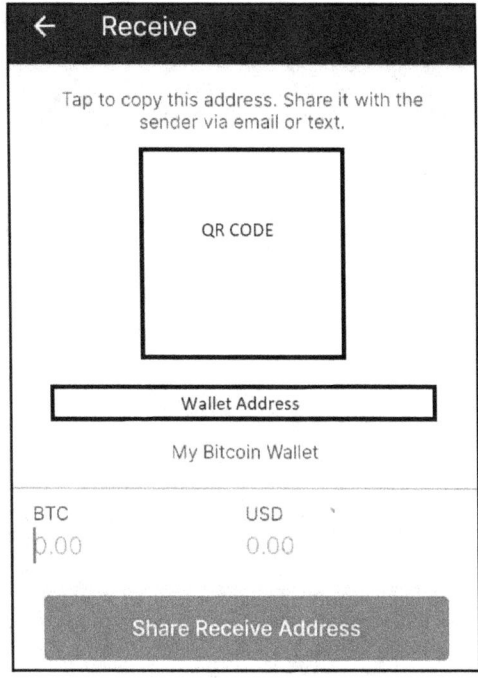

Step 7: To send assets, tap on 'Transfer', then on 'Send'—you will see a list of your assets. If you do not have any funds, you can tap on 'Buy Crypto' to make a purchase.

Blockchain.com Browser Wallet

Step 1: To get started, go to Blockchain.com and click on the "Get Started" button.

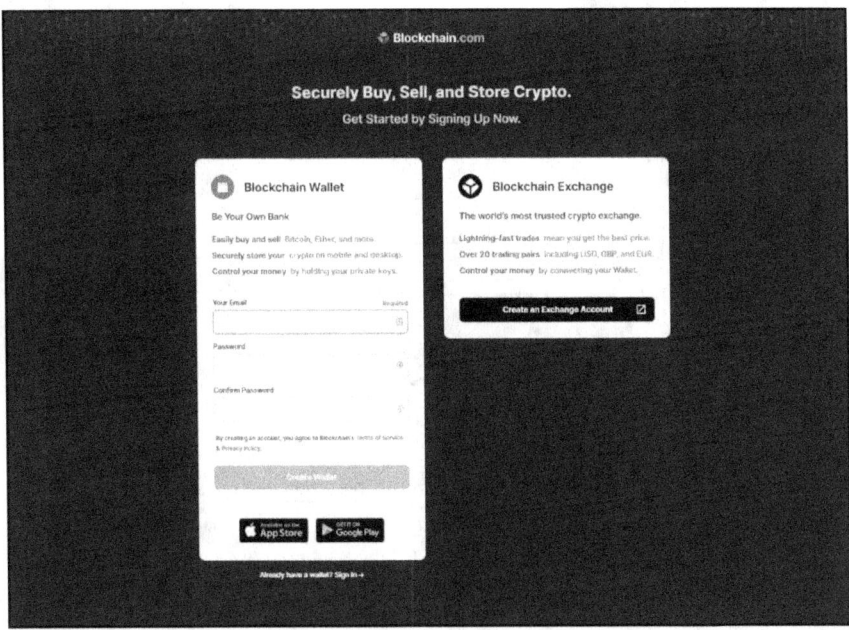

Step 2: Once logged in, the dashboard will show you coin balances in your wallet. To begin transferring funds to your Bitcoin wallet, click on 'Request'.

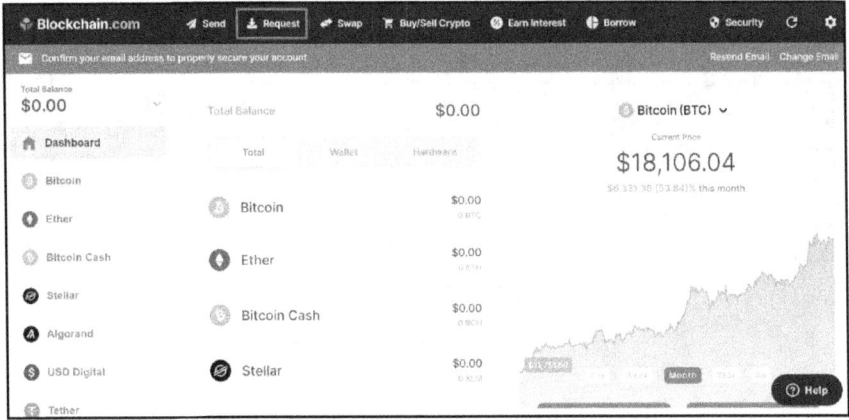

Step 3: Your bitcoin address will be shown. Be sure to double-check the address before making transactions.

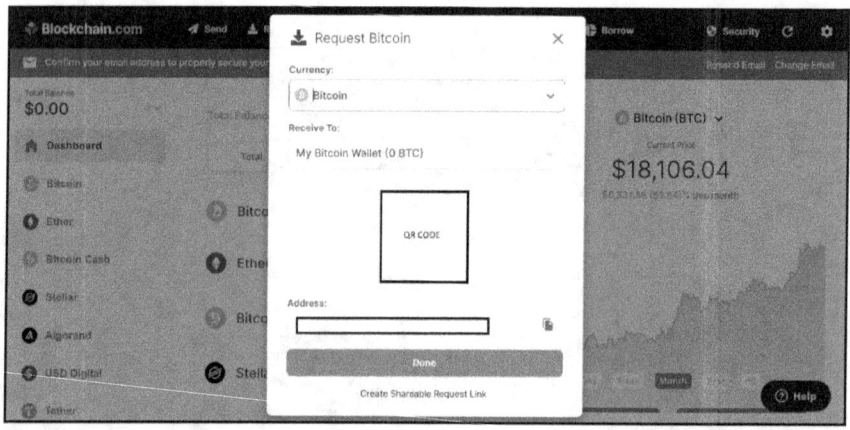

Step 4: To send bitcoin, click on the 'Send' button on the top menu bar. Insert the address you would like to send your funds to as well as the amount. You can also select the type of Network Fee. Regular is cheaper but slower while Priority is more expensive but results in faster confirmations.

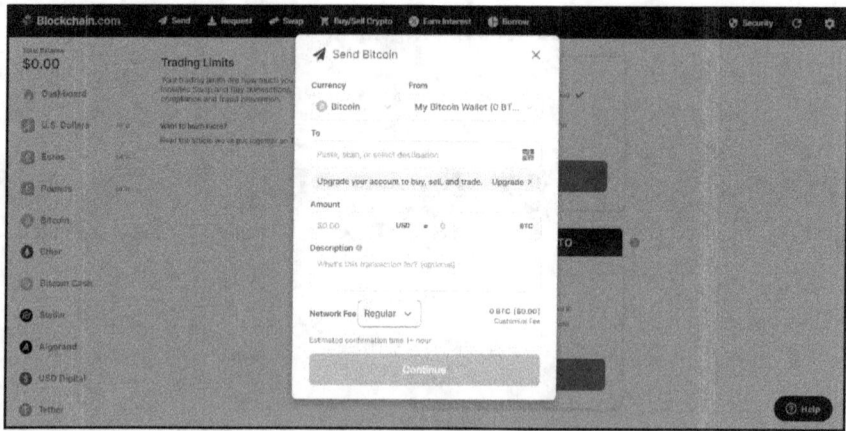

Lightning Network Wallets

Lightning wallets are essentially bitcoin wallets except that when you send and receive bitcoin, the transaction does not occur on the Bitcoin blockchain. Rather, it is routed through a second layer network built on top of the Bitcoin blockchain to facilitate instant and lower fee transactions. We will discuss further about Lightning Network in Chapter 8.

Lightning wallets are meant for instant and low-value transactions. One of the most user-friendly Lightning wallets you can try out is Phoenix Wallet by ACINQ, one of the pioneer firms in Lightning Network development.[71]

One very important point to note—Lightning Network is still considered experimental. Unlike the main Bitcoin blockchain that has been battle-tested for over a decade, bugs and software vulnerabilities may still exist.[72]

Due to the possibility that funds may be lost while transacting with Lightning Network, most Lightning wallets have implemented a limit on how much bitcoin you can store in them.

That being said, if you are looking to "buy coffee using bitcoin", a Lightning wallet is perfect for such a task. You would be surprised at just how seamless and instant it is to make transactions using Lightning Network.

---

[71] (n.d.). ACINQ | A Bitcoin Technology Company. Retrieved December 17, 2020, from https://acinq.co/

[72] "[Lightning-dev] Partial LND Vulnerability ... – Mailing Lists." 9 Oct. 2020, https://lists.linuxfoundation.org/pipermail/lightning-dev/2020-October/002819.html

Phoenix Wallet

Upon app installation, choose "create new wallet" and follow the steps provided in the app.

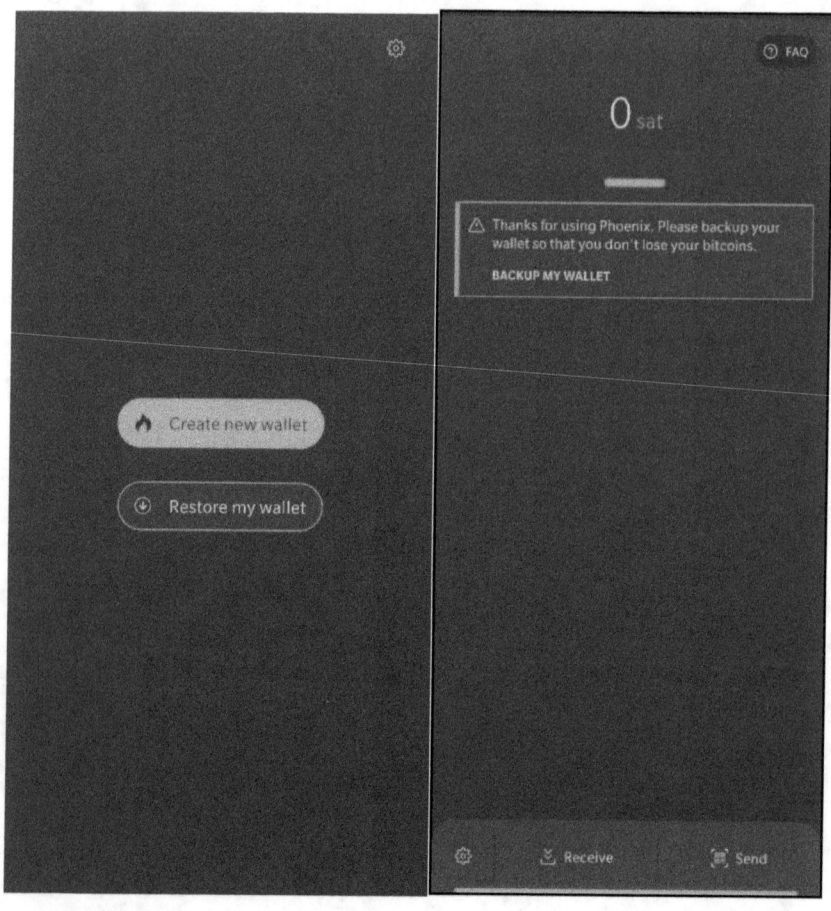

After the wallet is set up, you will be prompted to backup your wallet. Backing up your wallet ensures that you can still have access to your bitcoin in case you lost your smartphone or Lightning wallet app. Like any other bitcoin wallet, backing up involves writing down a set of random English words in a specific order—this is called the seed keys.

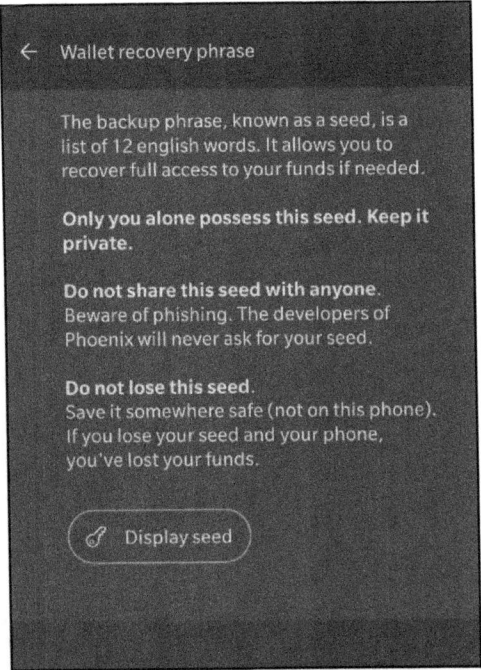

Important note: DO NOT store your seed keys online or even digitally. Write them down physically with a pen and notebook and store them in a place only you would know.

Once you have fully backed up your wallet, it is time to deposit your first bitcoin on the Lightning Network. Tap on the "Receive" button on the app to bring up the receive page and tap on "Show a Bitcoin Address". You can deposit funds to the newly generated bitcoin address.

Note that a small 0.1% Channel Opening fee will be applied to "migrate" your bitcoin onto the Lightning Network. You should not send too much bitcoin—anywhere between 0.0001 to 0.001 BTC (10,000 – 100,000 satoshis) should be more than enough to experiment with Lightning Network before trying out an even larger amount.

There is a hardcoded limit of 0.16 BTC at most Lightning wallets. Be careful not to reach the amount—if you need to send bitcoin above that quantity, it may be wise to use a standard bitcoin wallet instead of a Lightning wallet.

Step 4: To receive bitcoin via Lightning Network, let your sender scan the LN-URL QR code for them to initiate the transaction. You can also send the raw LN-URL link to the sender to initiate the transaction.

Fun Fact:
LN-URL always starts with **lnbc** followed by a long string of characters.

To send bitcoin, simply tap on the "Send" button to bring up the in-app QR scanner. When an LN-URL code is scanned, the payment page will pop up for you to set the amount of bitcoin you wish to send. Simply tap "Pay" once you are done and the funds will be sent immediately.

Lightning wallets are perfect for making small instant transactions using bitcoin when there is no need for your transaction to be mined and permanently stored on the blockchain forever.

If you would like to move your bitcoin from the Lightning Network back onto the Bitcoin blockchain, you can do so via an operation called "Closing channels". To do so, tap the "Settings" icon on the app and tap on the "Close all channels" option to bring up the close channel page.

You will need to prepare a destination bitcoin address when closing the channel. Simply tap "Empty my wallet" once you have pasted the bitcoin address to empty out your Lightning wallet fully.

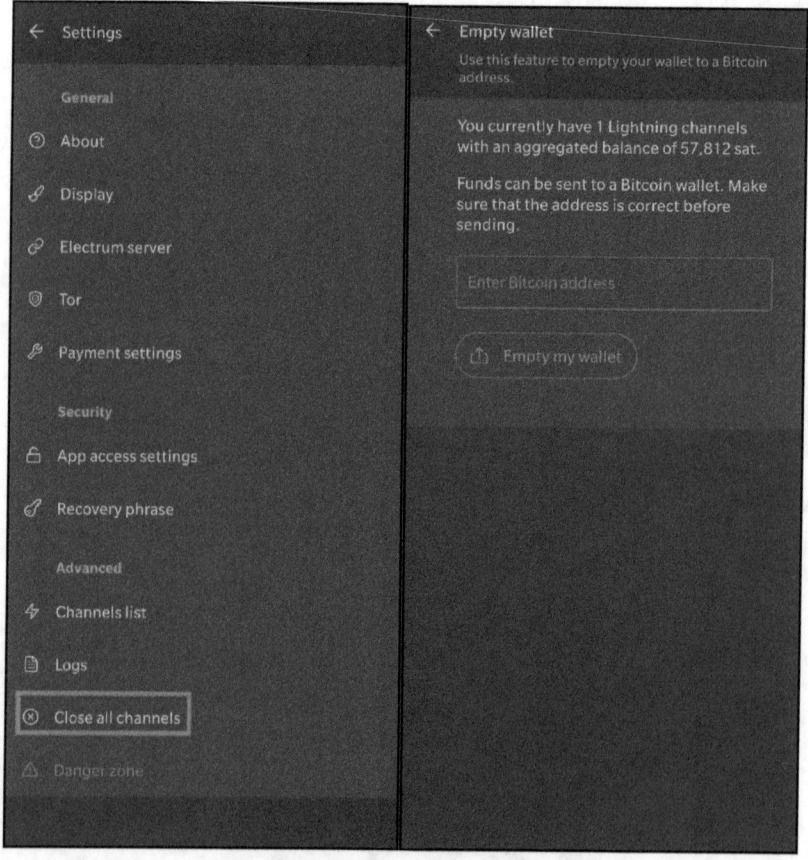

Alternative Lightning Wallets

Wallet of Satoshi

Wallet of Satoshi is another easy, out-of-the-box lightning wallets. Simply download the app and start sending and receiving Lightning Network payments. You are not required to create an account. Instead, your device acts as your ID, and as long as you do not delete the app or lose your phone you can continue using the wallet. There is also an option for you to sign up with an email address in order to back up your account.

Breez

Breez wallet is an open-source, non-custodial mobile wallet available on iOS and Android. It can help you open up a Lightning Network channel and it gives you full control over your funds.

Bluewallet

Bluewallet is a full-service user-friendly bitcoin wallet with Lightning Network support. This means you can both store regular on-chain Bitcoin as well as Lightning Network bitcoin in one app.

CHAPTER 7: ADVANCED BITCOIN WALLETS

If you made it this far, congratulations! But wait, we are only getting started. This chapter introduces some advanced Bitcoin topics such as running a full node and using special privacy techniques such as CoinJoin to send transactions.

This is not a chapter meant for beginners as it features very technical material and references.

Bitcoin Core Full Node

To really immerse yourself in the "Bitcoin experience", you might consider running a Bitcoin full node.

A full node is a program that fully validates transactions and blocks.[73] A Bitcoin full node keeps a complete copy of the Bitcoin blockchain and helps the network by accepting transactions and blocks from other full nodes, validating those transactions and blocks, and then relaying them to other full nodes.

You can think of the process of running your own Bitcoin full node as operating your own bank, where you are in charge of not only your own

---

[73] (n.d.). Running A Full Node – Bitcoin.org. Retrieved January 20, 2021, from https://bitcoin.org/en/full-node

funds but also actively puts on a check and balance role to ensure other banks are not involved with foul play. This is what bitcoin enthusiasts mean with the tagline "Be your own bank".

Full Node Requirements

Running a Bitcoin full node requires hardware of a certain specification for it to run smoothly. If your computer meets the following requirements, there should be no issue with running a full node:

- Desktop or laptop running recent versions of Windows, Mac OS X, or Linux.
- At least 400 GB of free hard disk space, accessible at a minimum read/write speed of 100 MB/s.
- At least 2 GB of RAM
- An Internet connection with upload speeds of at least 400 kilobits (50 kilobytes) per second
- An unmetered connection, or at the very least a connection with high upload/download quota. You need to download the whole 300-400 GB of blockchain data upon first installation, and may relay at least 20-30 GB of network data a month as a full node.
- At least 6 hours a day where your full node can be left running in the background. Ideally, you should run the full node continuously at all times.

When running a Bitcoin full node, you may want to obscure your digital footprint and increase your network privacy by using a Virtual Private Network (VPN) service or other network obfuscation techniques.

If you are not careful, a full node that regularly broadcasts network information to other nearby nodes may expose your identity and location. You may also want to consider operating a full node using a dedicated device solely for this purpose.

Download

For the purpose of demonstration, we will install the most widely used Bitcoin full node implementation—known as Bitcoin Core, on a Windows Operating System.[74]

---

[74] (n.d.). About – Bitcoin Core. Retrieved January 20, 2021, from

The quickest way to download the software is via the link at Bitcoin.org/en/download. It may be helpful to compare the versions in Bitcoin's Github repository (https://github.com/bitcoin/bitcoin/releases) as that is where the bitcoin full node software will be first released with every new update before being made available from other download sources.[75]

In this case, we will download the "**bitcoin-0.20.1-win64-setup.exe**" version of the installation file.

Once you have downloaded the software, it is highly recommended that you verify the digital signature of the software before installing it.[76] You can do so via the "Verify release signatures" link which will let you download an ASCII file with the signatures encoded.

Take note of 3 things:
- The hashing algorithm used, from the "Hash" property
- The version of the installation software that you have downloaded
- The digital signature itself, which appears as a string of random numbers

---

https://bitcoincore.org/en/about/
[75] (n.d.). Releases · bitcoin/bitcoin · GitHub. Retrieved January 20, 2021, from https://github.com/bitcoin/bitcoin/releases
[76] (n.d.). Digital signature – Wikipedia. Retrieved January 20, 2021, from https://en.wikipedia.org/wiki/Digital_signature

To verify the digital signature of the software, right-click on the installation file to click "Properties" and open up the properties page and click "Security". Copy the "Object name", also known as the "file path", of the file in full.

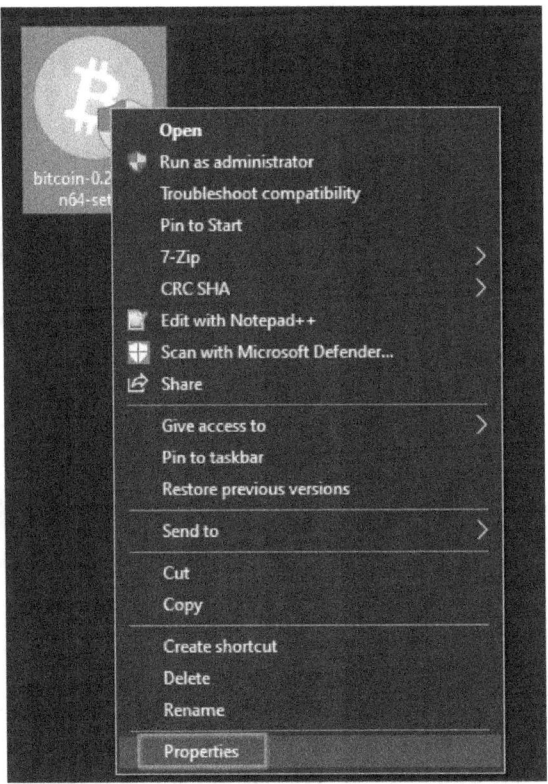

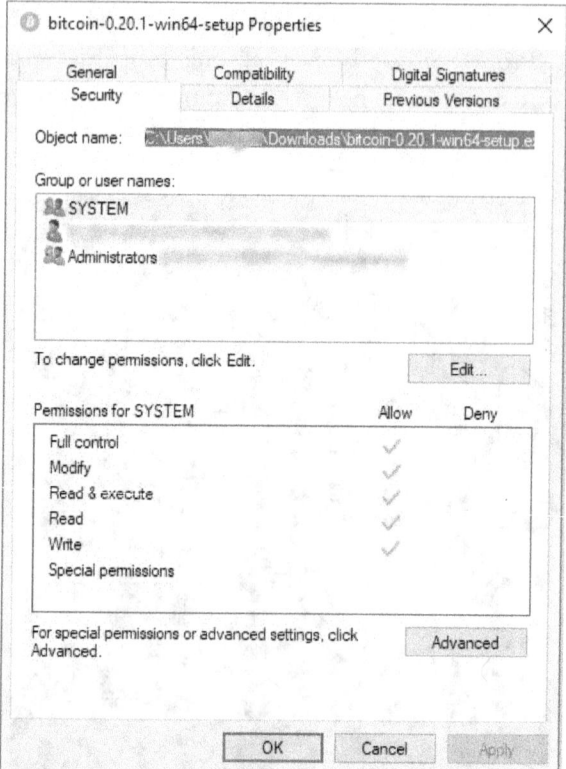

In this case, it should look like

C:\Users\pc-name\Downloads\bitcoin-0.20.1-win64-setup.exe

"pc name" would be the name of your computer, whereas "Downloads" would be the Downloads folder where your downloaded files are stored. Your file path may differ depending on how you have set up your computer.

Next, open up Windows Command Prompt terminal. In the Command Prompt, enter the following commands

Certutil -hashfile C:\Users\pc-name\Downloads\bitcoin-0.20.1-win64-setup.exe SHA256

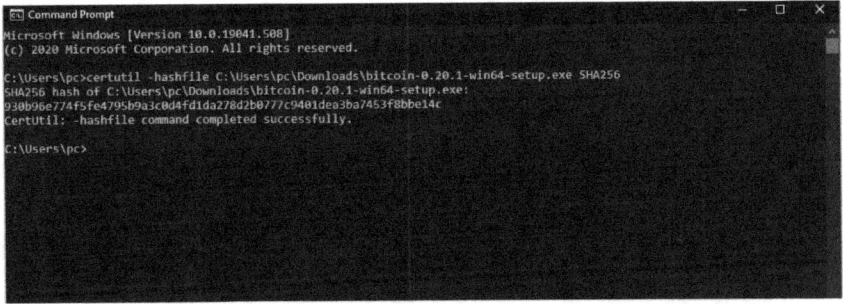

> **Fun Fact:**
> "**Certutil**" refers to Microsoft's own preinstalled digital signatures software.
> "**-hashfile**" refers to the command to cryptographically hash the file you inserted, which will result in a digital signature.
> "**SHA256**" refers to the hashing algorithm you instruct the software to hash the file with.
> You might notice the algorithm has the same name as the one used in the Bitcoin Protocol. This is because they indeed are the same hashing algorithm.

Finally, compare the resulting hash within the command prompt with the one provided from the website. If the digital signature is the same, the software has not been altered in any way from the source as it downloads into your computer.

Installation

Installation of Bitcoin Core is fairly straightforward. Follow the instructions on the screen and wait for the installation to proceed. Once the installation has been completed, you will be greeted with Bitcoin Core's welcome page.

This where you can customize the settings for the full node—where the blockchain data is stored in your computer and whether you want to prune the blockchain data (deleting the data after your full node has verified them, this will no longer deactivate Bitcoin Core as a full node on your computer).

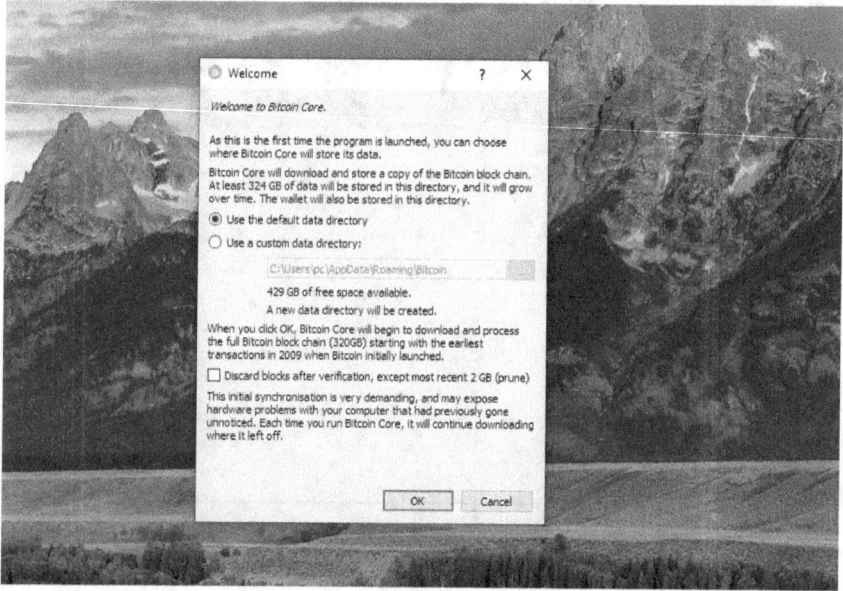

Once you have clicked on the "OK" button, the initial download of blockchain data will immediately commence.

> **Note**: Downloading the initial blockchain data is a very demanding task for your hardware. Not only will your computer need to download the data via Bitcoin's P2P network (similar to torrenting), your computer will verify the downloaded data independently—a task heavy in calculation.

Downloading the Bitcoin Blockchain

Now comes the waiting game. Bitcoin Core will now proceed to download the entirety of bitcoin's blockchain, block by block, into your computer. This is known as "Initial Block Download".[77] It is wise to leave your computer running for the download while you are not using it.

It is fine to shut down the Bitcoin Core program while it is still downloading, if you need to use your computer for something else. The block download will resume the next time you open the program.

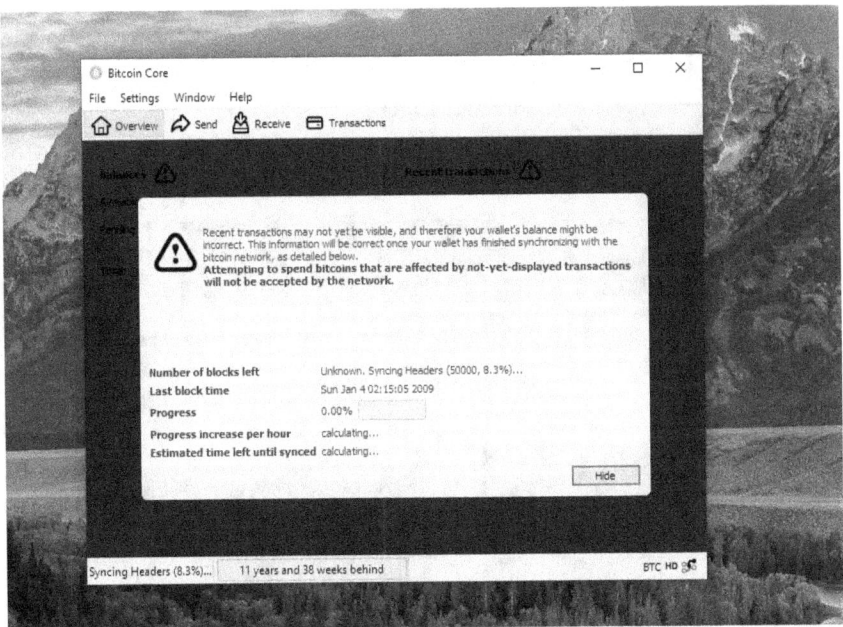

Network Traffic Chart

Clicking on "Window > Network Traffic" opens up the Network Traffic Chart, which shows live upload/download statistics while the Bitcoin Core program is running. It may be helpful to monitor your internet data usage if it is a concern to you.

---

[77] (n.d.). P2P Network – Bitcoin.org. Retrieved January 20, 2021, from
https://developer.bitcoin.org/devguide/p2p_network.html

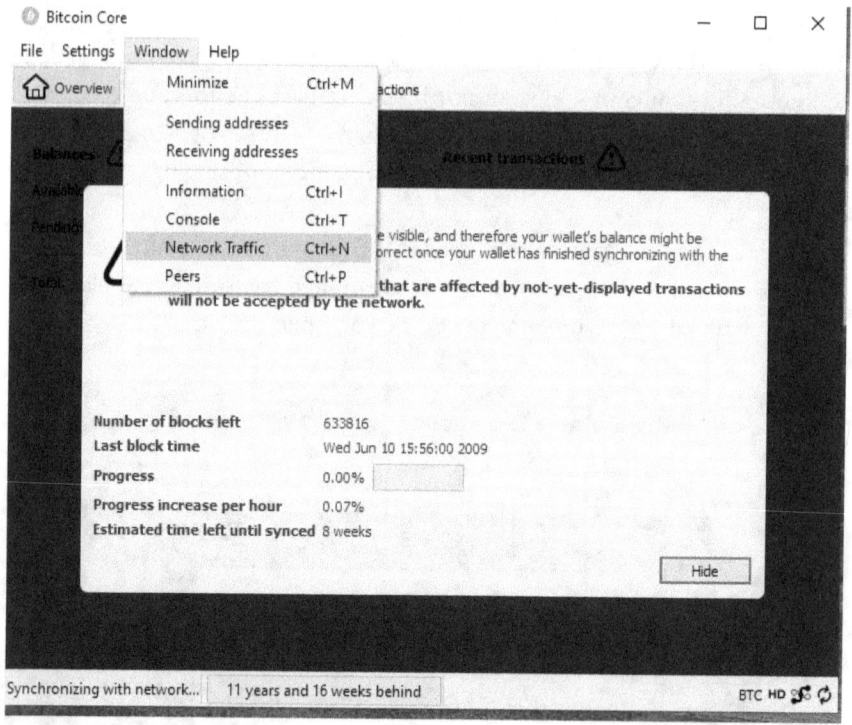

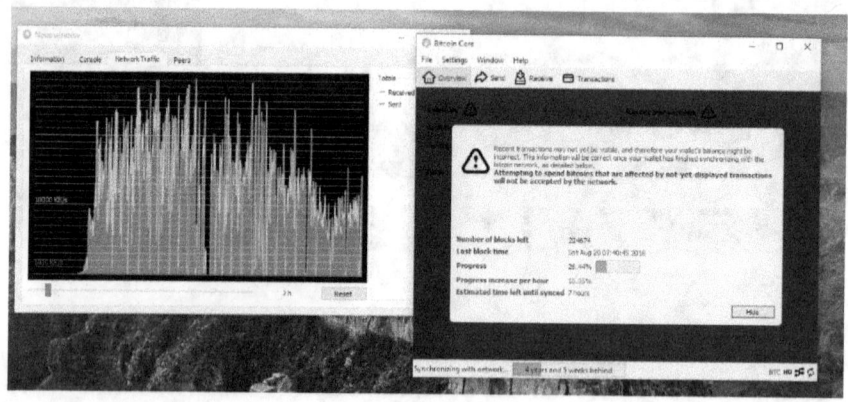

Note: Synchronizing the blockchain is a time-consuming activity. You are downloading up to 350GB of data from peer-to-peer nodes that are connected to you.

Using Bitcoin Core Full Node as a Wallet

Some time may have passed before the initial block download. Once it is done, congratulations! You are now part of a global network of Bitcoin nodes and actively making the Bitcoin Network more robust.[78] [79]

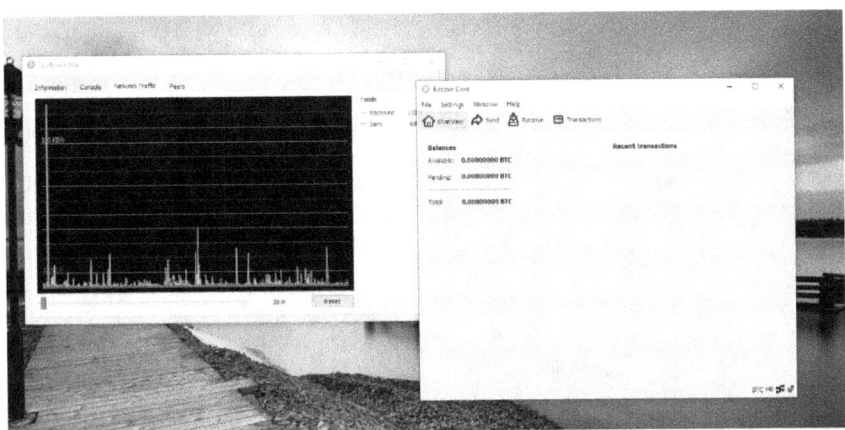

Now that you have fully downloaded the bitcoin blockchain, you can start sending and receiving bitcoin using Bitcoin Core. Using the Bitcoin Full Node is the most baseline way of sending and receiving bitcoin. In the very early days of Bitcoin, this was the only way to send and receive bitcoin.

Receiving Bitcoin

To receive bitcoin on your full node, simply click on the "Receive" button. You can generate a new bitcoin address by clicking "Create a new receiving address".

You can label the address, enter the amount requested, and even attach a message in the address. Doing so will generate a request payment QR code for your sender to easily scan and send the bitcoin to.

---

[78] (n.d.). Bitnodes. Retrieved January 20, 2021, from https://bitnodes.io/
[79] (2019, October 24). Why Run a Node? – Casa Blog. Retrieved January 20, 2021, from https://blog.keys.casa/why-run-a-node/

Important note: Always generate a new bitcoin address every time you want to receive payment. Reusing an address presents a privacy risk to yourself as hackers may be able to trace your transactions and cause harm to you.

Sending Bitcoin

To send bitcoin, simply open up the "Send" page and enter the bitcoin address and amount you want to send to. Labeling the bitcoin address allows for easier reference the next time you want to send bitcoin to that same address.

You can also adjust the transaction fee you wish to pay (valued in sats per bytes) for the transaction. Do note that the less you pay, the longer your transaction will likely take to be mined by miners as miners tend to prioritize transactions with higher transaction fees.

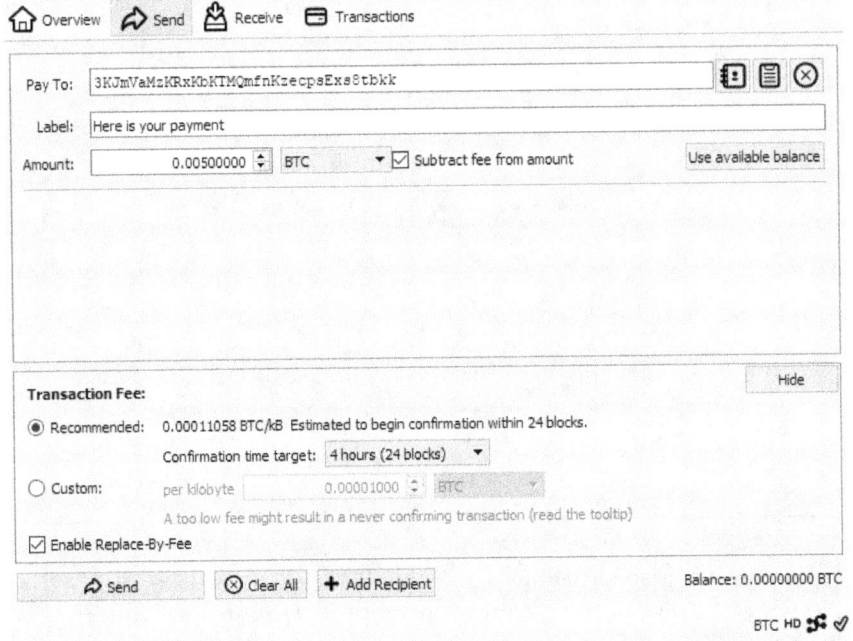

Using the Bitcoin Full Node Console

As the name suggests, a Bitcoin Full Node does more than just sending and receiving bitcoin. Because a full node stores the entirety of the bitcoin blockchain, you can query all sorts of blockchain data to get the latest information about the bitcoin blockchain.[81] Simply access the Bitcoin console by clicking "Windows > Console" to open up the console.

Some of the example data you can query includes the latest bitcoin mining statistics, data in a certain block, network information on the bitcoin full nodes that are connected to you, and even all the pending transactions that are currently queued for mining by the miners.

Here is an example of one of the queries you can call with the console named **gettxoutsetinfo**.

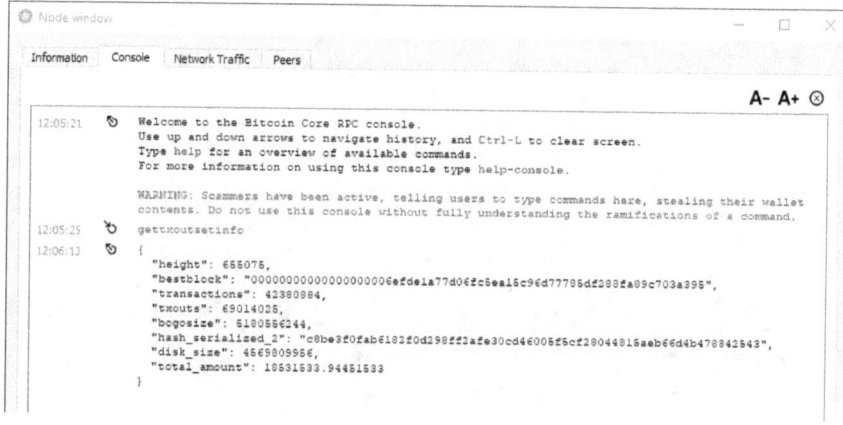

> **Fun Fact:**
> Even though **gettxoutsetinfo** is a relatively basic query, there are already a few very useful pieces of information presented. Here are what some of the data means:
> Height = number of the latest bitcoin block
> Transactions = number of transactions made on the blockchain
> Txout = number utxo currently on the blockchain

[80] (n.d.). Fee Estimates – Statoshi. Retrieved January 20, 2021, from https://statoshi.info/dashboard/db/fee-estimates

[81] (n.d.). Basic commands to interact with the Bitcoin Core RPC console. Retrieved January 20, 2021, from https://medium.com/@peterjd42/basic-commands-to-interact-with-the-bitcoin-core-rpc-console-180da2c2dc45

> Disk_size = The size of the blockchain in bytes
> Total_amount = circulating supply bitcoin

Samourai Mobile Wallet

To fully experience bitcoin's privacy features and capability on the go, you can consider using the Samourai Wallet as part of your bitcoin toolkit.

While there is a laundry list of bitcoin-dedicated mobile wallets out there—and even bitcoin-supported crypto wallets, none of them can rival Samourai Wallet in terms of features.[82]

Unlike typical mobile wallets that send bitcoin transactions in a straightforward manner, Samourai Wallet is developed with the philosophy towards "creating the software that Silicon Valley will never build, the regulators will never allow, and the VCs will never invest in".[83]

Various features such as Paynym[84], Stonewall[85] and Whirlpool[86] makes bitcoin transactions much more resilient to stalkers who track your transactions. One highlight is its CoinJoin capability, which we will describe in Chapter 8. Even if you do not plan to use these features, knowing the options readily available is always a good thing.

Installation

Step 1: The best place to find the download link for Samourai Wallet is via their official website's download page.[87] You can either download the APK files directly or head to the Google Play Store page. If you choose to download the APK files, be sure to also verify the digital signature with the ones provided by the Samourai team.

---

[82] (n.d.). Feature Comparison – Samourai Wallet. Retrieved December 17, 2020, from https://samouraiwallet.com/features/comparison

[83] (n.d.). Samourai Wallet – Features. Retrieved December 17, 2020, from https://samouraiwallet.com/features

[84] (n.d.). Bitcoin Q&A: Samourai, Wasabi, and privacy on Huffduffer. Retrieved December 17, 2020, from https://huffduffer.com/uwefassnacht/544981

[85] (n.d.). STONEWALL – Samourai Wallet. Retrieved December 17, 2020, from https://samouraiwallet.com/stonewall

[86] (n.d.). Whirlpool – Samourai Wallet. Retrieved December 17, 2020, from https://samouraiwallet.com/whirlpool

[87] (n.d.). Download – Samourai Wallet. Retrieved December 17, 2020, from https://samouraiwallet.com/download

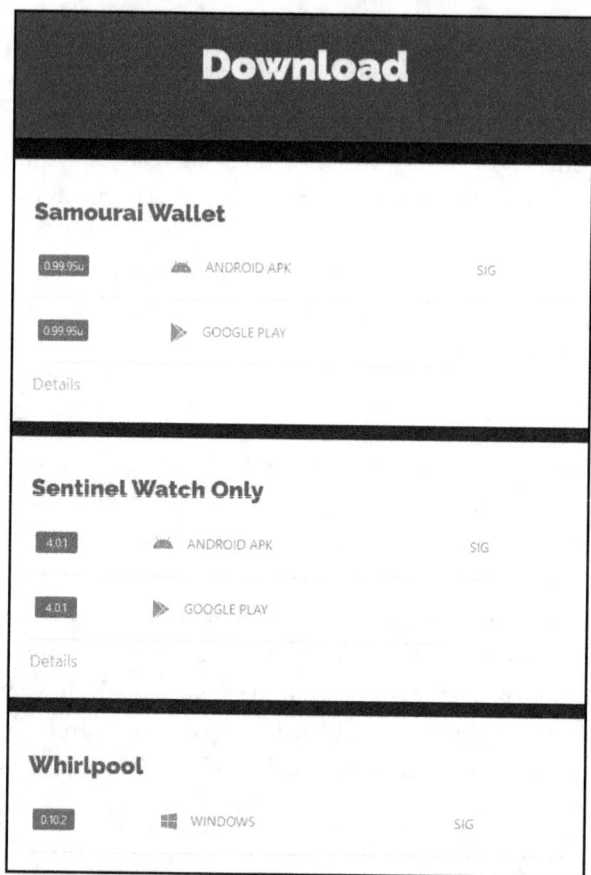

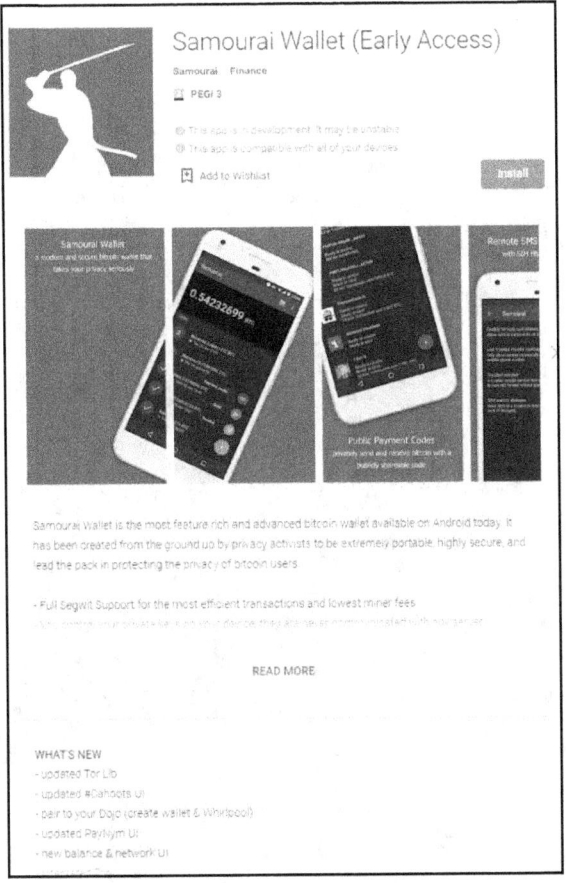

Setting Up

Step 2: Install the app on your Android smartphone and follow the set-up guide. Samourai Wallet comes with an in-built TOR (the onion router) anonymity network to allow you to broadcast your bitcoin transaction on the TOR network.[88]

Enabling TOR when using Samourai offers another set of anonymity advantages on top of the privacy tools you will use within the app.

---

[88] (n.d.). Tor (anonymity network) – Wikipedia. Retrieved January 20, 2021, from https://en.wikipedia.org/wiki/Tor_(anonymity_network)

Step 3: Write down your passphrase, PIN and the 12-word mnemonic keys.

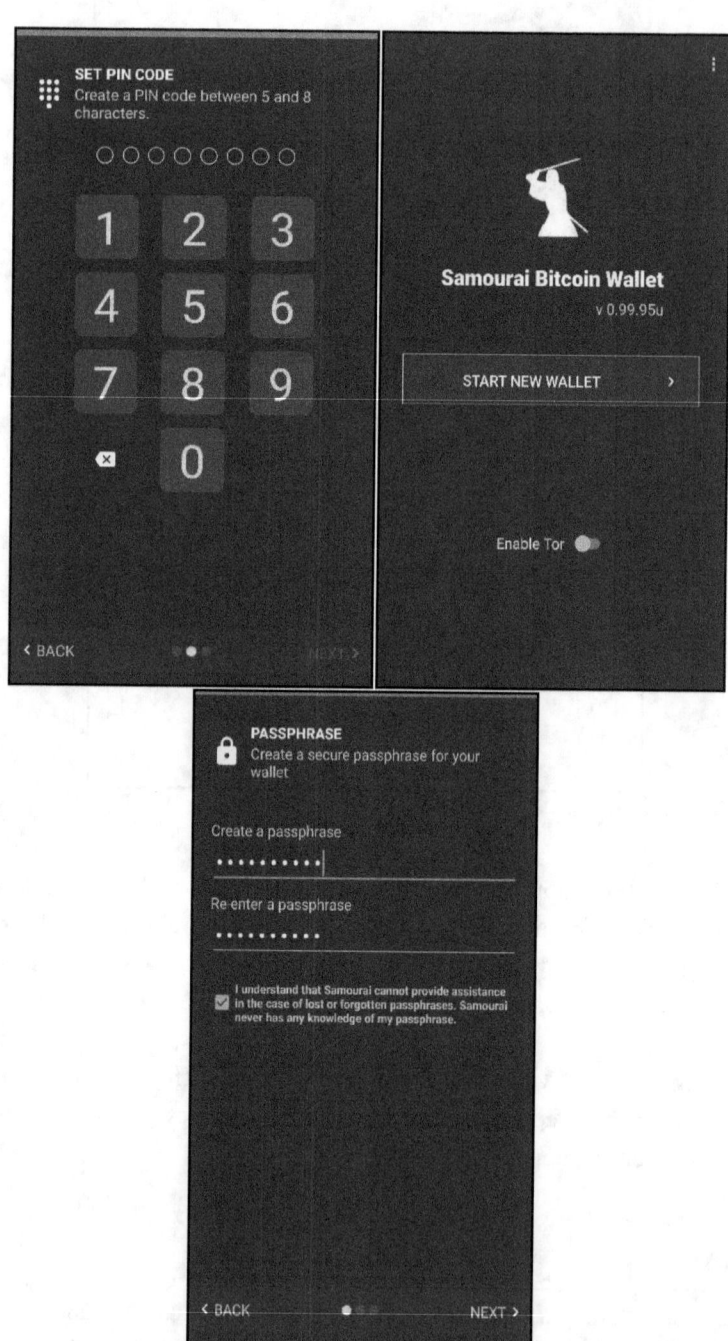

Receiving Bitcoin

Step 4: You have now successfully completed the set-up for the Samourai mobile wallet and be able to view the main screen, where various functions are available. Tapping on the menu at the bottom right of the screen will bring up Whirlpool, PayNyms, Send, and Receive.

Step 5: To receive bitcoin, simply tap on the "Receive" icon and send your address to the sender. Alternatively, get them to scan your QR code.

Step 6: To customize your receiving address, tap on the "Advanced" icon, which will let you choose the type of bitcoin address you want to generate or even create a bitcoin payment request for a specific amount.

Note: "SegWit native" addresses are typically the best option for bitcoin payments due to lower fees and more flexibility to apply privacy features through Samourai Wallet.

Sending Bitcoin

Step 7: Sending bitcoin through Samourai Wallet gives you great flexibility in choosing the types of on-chain privacy features that you want for your transaction. Tap on the "Send" icon from the main page to go to the Send page.

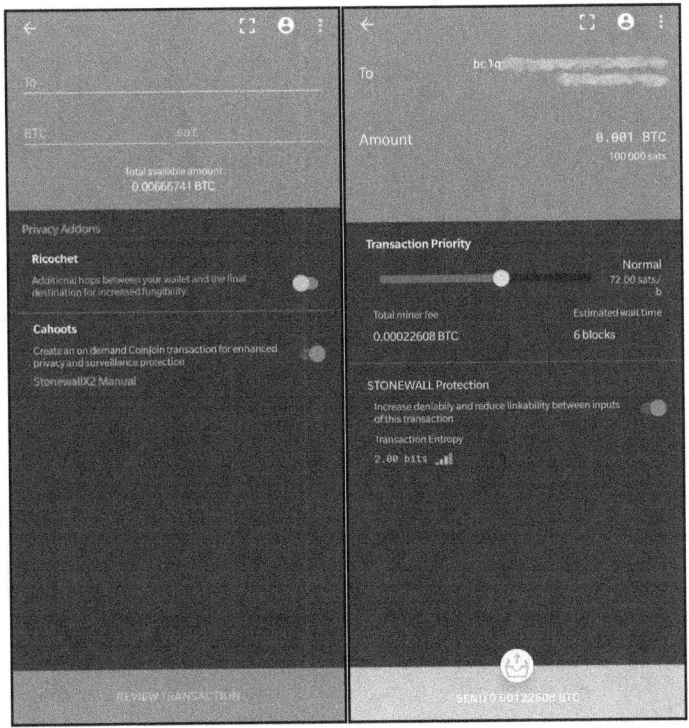

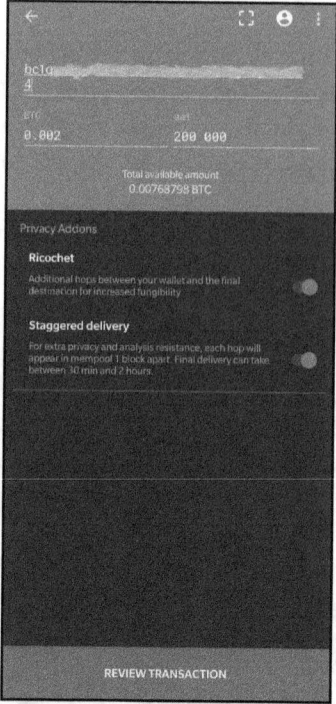

Here's a quick primer of the various privacy features and how they affect the transaction:

- Ricochet = Several "fake transactions" or Hops will be made before the bitcoin reaches your destination address. This feature is to fool outside observers into thinking the bitcoin has passed many hands, breaking the linkage between the sender and receiver.
- Staggered delivery = A modification of Ricochet, where there will be a time delay between each Hop to further trick outside observers.
- Stonewall = A "fake" CoinJoin transaction between the sender and receiver to make it harder for an outside observer to determine which address sends how much bitcoin. This transaction tricks the stalker into thinking the transaction involves more than two parties.
- Cahoot = Collaborative Transaction,[89] These transaction types require both the sender and receiver to actively set up a CoinJoin transaction.

---

[89] (2019, March 11). Samourai Wallet — Collaborative Transactions – "Cahoots". Retrieved January 20, 2021, from https://blog.samouraiwallet.com/post/183378923792/collaborative-transactions-cahoots

Samourai Whirlpool (CoinJoin)

At its core, CoinJoin is a trustless method for combining multiple Bitcoin payments from multiple spenders into a single transaction to make it more difficult for outside parties to determine which spender paid which recipients. CoinJoin transactions do not require a modification to the bitcoin protocol, meaning it can be done on the bitcoin blockchain itself.

Samourai Whirlpool is one such CoinJoin implementation that allows users to execute a CoinJoin transaction in an easy-to-use manner.

Step 1: To perform a CoinJoin, tap on the menu button followed by "Whirlpool".

This will bring you to the Whirlpool screen. Since no CoinJoin transaction has been performed, the balance is null. Tap on the "Whirlpool" icon on the bottom right to continue.

Terms Recap:
UTXO = your bitcoin (basically)
Premix = bitcoin that has not gone through Whirlpool mixing.
Postmix = bitcoin that has already been mixed through Whirlpool.

Advanced Bitcoin Wallets

You will now be prompted to either "Mix UTXOs" or "Spend Mixed UTXOs". Tap on the "Mix UTXOs" button to proceed.

The balance in your wallet will be displayed. You can select which UXTO set you will want to add into the mix.

Due to Samourai Whirlpool's implementation limits, mixing bitcoin on Whirlpool's Coinjoin is limited to a set of fixed numbers (0.01, 0.05 and 0.5). Every participant must put in the same amount of bitcoin for Coinjoin to work.

Think of it as buying a ticket for fresh money where the ticket price is the same as the money you will receive at the end of the day. Therefore, every participant who wishes to join the mixing must pay the same amount as per the price of the ticket.

Select the pool you would like to join depending on your balance. In this example, we went with the 0.01 BTC pool. The cycle priority will determine the speed of the mixing.

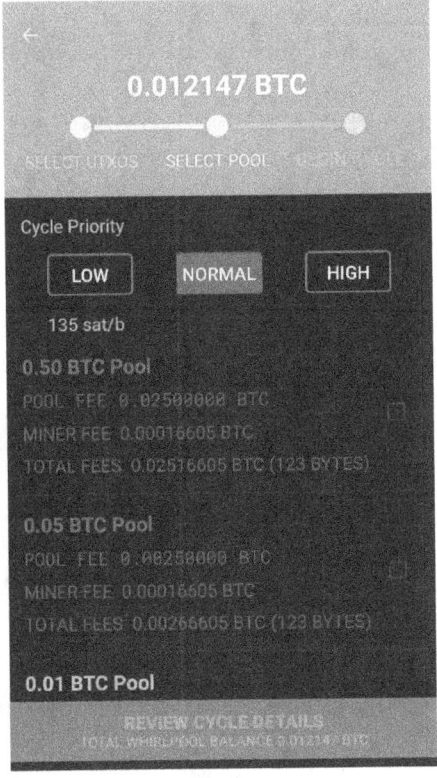

Once you have selected the pool, you may begin the CoinJoin process.

Keep in mind that you only need to pay a one-time fee to begin the Whirlpool cycle. However, once your bitcoin is mixing, you can enjoy infinite amounts of mix as long as you do not withdraw from the Whirlpool.

Just before the process begins, a popup notification will prompt you to block the "Doxxic Change" from being spent in your wallet. It is a good idea to tap "YES" to allow Samourai wallet to tag the Doxxic bitcoin.

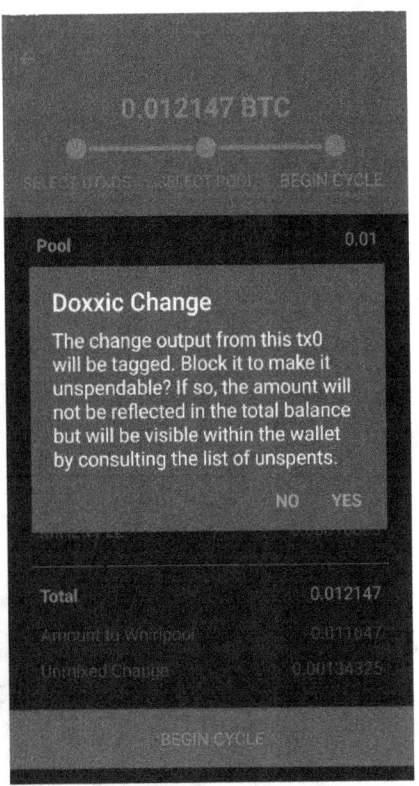

Important note: "Doxxic", a portmanteau of "dox"[90] and "toxic", are "remainder" bitcoin from the addresses where you originally draw the bitcoin from. Because the bitcoin comes from the same address, it is possible for outside observers to link your postmix bitcoin to your original premix address[91]. This will defeat the purpose of the CoinJoin.

[90] (n.d.). Doxing – Wikipedia. Retrieved January 20, 2021, from
https://en.wikipedia.org/wiki/Doxing
[91] (2020, June 15). Dealing with Coinjoin Change Outputs – Bitcoin Q+A. Retrieved January 20, 2021, from https://www.bitcoinqna.com/post/dealing-with-coinjoin-change-outputs

The transaction will enter the queue and start mixing. Due to current limitations of Whirlpool implementation, the Samourai wallet app can only proceed while it is running on your smartphone.[92]

Imagine Whirlpool as a laundry machine which only runs if it is online. As a rule of thumb, it is best to leave the whirlpool running as long as possible for maximum effectiveness. Whirlpool will continue to mix with each incoming participant into the pool, which further increases the anonymity of your postmix bitcoin.

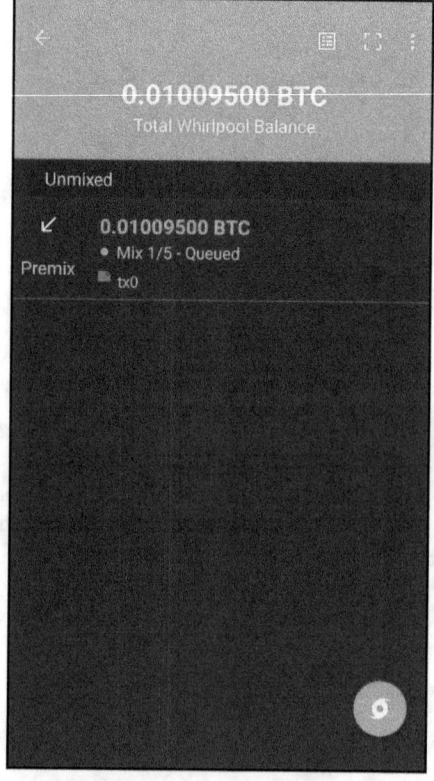

---

[92] More advanced users may run a Dojo or Whirlpool Desktop app to monitor their whirlpool mixes offline.

Mixing is now complete and is ready to be spent. There's also the option to add notes to the transaction. We labelled ours "Mixed BTC".

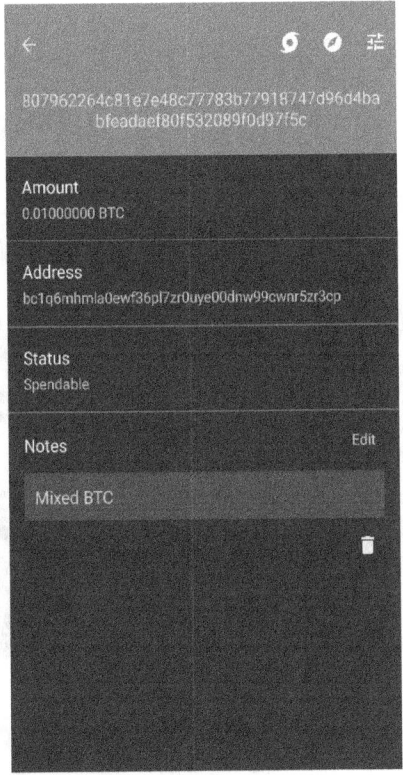

To access your "Mixed BTC", simply head to the home screen and tap on the Samourai icon on the top left corner.

This will be your mixed balance that you will be able to send to other wallets by tapping on the bottom right corner icon.

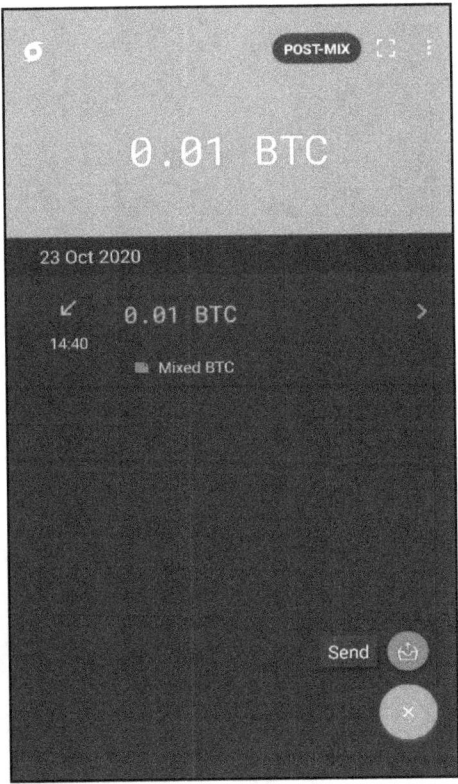

Congratulations, you have successfully performed a CoinJoin transaction.

PART 3: THE FUTURE OF BITCOIN

CHAPTER 8: BITCOIN'S IMPROVEMENTS

Despite being the most well-known and valuable cryptocurrency in the world, Bitcoin is not without complications. Scalability issues arising from code and hardware limitations plagued the network since inception, hindering it from becoming a highly efficient and viable global payment system.

Conversely, Bitcoin community members and developers have worked together over the years to improve the Bitcoin protocol in various ways. In this chapter, we will take a closer look at some of the main problems faced by Bitcoin users and the solutions devised to solve them.

Scalability

Bitcoin's scalability issues is one of the most-frequently debated topics by bitcoin developers and community members. Compared to Visa's payment network which can allegedly handle approximately 24,000 transactions per second, Bitcoin's network can only handle an average of 7 transactions per second.[93] This represents a major obstacle in its path to global adoption as an alternative payment system.

---

[93] (n.d.) What Is Lightning Network And How It Works – Cointelegraph. Retrieved November 17, 2020, from https://cointelegraph.com/lightning-network-101/what-is-lightning-network-and-how-it-works

Two commonly cited efforts solutions to improve Bitcoin scalability are Segregated Witness (SegWit) and Lightning Network (LN).

Segregated Witness (SegWit)

> By removing some data out of each Bitcoin transaction, you can pack more transactions into each block (every 10 minute) and therefore achieve higher transaction throughput.

Bitcoin was programmed with a block size cap of 1MB per block. With each transaction taking up roughly 250 bytes of space, the only way for more transactions to be processed every 10 minutes is by increasing block size or reducing transaction size.

The SegWit proposal sets out to reduce transaction size by segregating digital signatures outside of the block on the Bitcoin blockchain. This would free up roughly 60% of a Bitcoin's block space, allowing more transactions to be packed in a block. The SegWit proposal was given the green light by the community as per the New York Agreement (NYA) and included as part of BIP 141.[94]

Removing the digital signature outside of each transaction does not affect a transaction, as the effect of each transaction is determined by the output, or how much and where it is spent. The digital signature is only required to validate the transaction on the blockchain, but not to determine it.

With that in mind, Dr Peter Wuille, a Bitcoin developer, proposed an upgrade of the Bitcoin protocol known as Segregated Witness, or SegWit for short. Digital signatures take up more than half the space in a transaction and SegWit attempts to segregate the signature from the input by moving it towards the end of the transaction. This reduction in required block space per transaction allowed for an increase in maximum theoretical block capacity from 1MB to 4MB.

---

[94] (2017, June 20). Bitcoin Miners Are Signaling Support for the New York .... Retrieved January 19, 2021, from https://bitcoinmagazine.com/articles/miners-are-signaling-support-new-york-agreement-heres-what-means

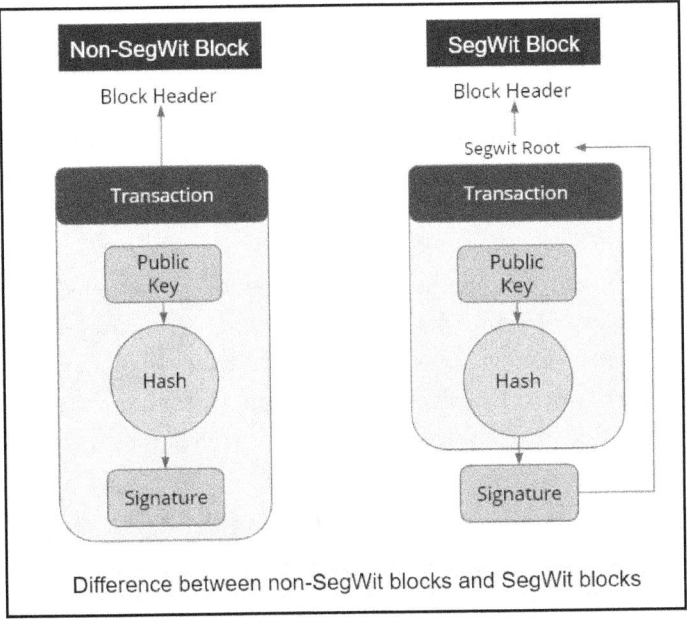

Difference between non-SegWit blocks and SegWit blocks

On 24 August 2017, SegWit was successfully included into the Bitcoin protocol as a soft-fork and the throughput for the Bitcoin network increased from 3 transactions per second to 7 transactions per second.

Additionally, SegWit also fixed what is known as transaction malleability, where transactions can be tweaked to "look" different without actually affecting the underlying amount transacted. Resolving this paved the way for the development of layer two protocols like the Lightning Network, which we will be covering next.

Lightning Network (LN)

> By processing transactions on a second layer which allows for faster and cheaper transactions without burdening the main Bitcoin layer, Lightning Network has the potential to solve Bitcoin's scaling issues. Note that Lightning Network is still a work in progress initiative as of December 2020.

Although SegWit has improved Bitcoin's capabilities in processing transactions, it is just one of the many solutions that have been proposed to allow the network to compete with the incumbent payment giants. One of the more interesting features that have received much attention is Lightning Network (LN), a proposed and experimental scalability solution to address some of the potential problems on the Bitcoin Network as more users inevitably use and congest the network[95].

By design, bitcoin transactions are overwhelmingly immutable and secure. Once a transaction is broadcasted to the Bitcoin Network, thousands of miners and nodes will compute, hash, and store the data immutably on the blockchain. However, this also makes it inconvenient for simple payments like buying coffee or giving tips to online content creators.

Simply put, the Lighting Network was envisioned as a second-layer settlement network built on top of the Bitcoin Network. It is a scalable, instant and efficient payment system focused on small transactions that can be consolidated into fewer transactions before being broadcasted onto the Bitcoin Network.

With Lightning Network, transactions are processed on the second layer network and ultimately verified on the main blockchain. Not only does this help reduce the on-chain traffic, it also helps to reduce inflated fees caused by overloaded transactions, since numerous transactions can now be recorded as a single transaction on the main blockchain. It has been said that Lightning Network can theoretically handle up to 1 million transactions per second, miles ahead of Bitcoin's 7 transactions per second.

The philosophy that creates Lightning Network was as old as Bitcoin itself. In fact, Satoshi Nakamoto drafted the codes for what would eventually be a way to move bitcoin between the Lightning Network from the Bitcoin blockchain.

---

[95] (n.d.) What Is Lightning Network And How It Works – Cointelegraph. Retrieved November 17, 2020, from https://cointelegraph.com/lightning-network-101/what-is-lightning-network-and-how-it-works

```
// Check for conflicts with in-memory transactions
CTransaction* ptxOld = NULL;
for (int i = 0; i < vin.size(); i++)
{
    COutPoint outpoint = vin[i].prevout;
    if (mapNextTx.count(outpoint))
    {
        // Allow replacing with a newer version of the same transaction
        if (i != 0)
            return false;
        ptxOld = mapNextTx[outpoint].ptx;
        if (!IsNewerThan(*ptxOld))
            return false;
        for (int i = 0; i < vin.size(); i++)
```

A code blob in the Bitcoin Code originally written by Nakamoto that would be the basis for Lightning Network. Source: historical repository of Satoshi Nakamoto's original bitcoin source code

Lightning Network payments are nearly instantaneous and have extremely low fees, opening up many possibilities and is one of the many qualities required to be a viable global payments system.

One very interesting experiment that was done earlier was the Lightning Torch, where an amount of satoshis would be sent to a trusted user, or 'torchbearer'. It would continue on and on until a malicious actor decides not to pass on the torch. Experiments like this quickly became a testing ground for the earliest versions of Lightning Network. The most popular variation was started by a pseudonymous Twitter user called hodlonaut, which quickly grew into a global phenomenon.[96]

However, as of December 2020, the LN is still considered to be in development and not yet fully operational. Teams such as ACINQ, Blockstream and Lightning Labs are still hard at work to develop their own versions of LN, but no one can ensure that they would be fully functional and bug-free so users will still have to wait.

---

[96] (2019, February 5). Bitcoin's 'Lightning Torch' Explained: What It Is and ... – CoinDesk. Retrieved January 20, 2021, from https://www.coindesk.com/bitcoins-lightning-torch-has-blazed-through-37-countries-so-far

Privacy

Another major concern for Bitcoin is privacy. While addresses themselves do not contain any personally identifiable information, all transactions are public, traceable, and stored permanently on the Bitcoin blockchain.

Since users have to reveal themselves when they transact, they may be putting their entire transaction history for people who want to look into it. While good practices such as using a new address for each payment can help, it does not fully solve the problem and Bitcoin payments are still not quite private.

CoinJoin

Although Bitcoin has been known for allowing users to make transactions anonymously, it is not entirely private to parties who know what to look for. Transactions can still be tracked using your Bitcoin address and therefore users do not remain completely anonymous.

This is where CoinJoin becomes a privacy game-changer for the Bitcoin protocol. Proposed by Greg Maxwell, a Bitcoin Core developer,[97] CoinJoin merges multiple payments from different spenders into a single transaction, making it indistinguishable from regular transactions.[98] This makes it more difficult for external observers to determine the recipients of a specific payment. As an added bonus to utility and convenience, CoinJoin does not require any upgrade of the existing Bitcoin protocol.

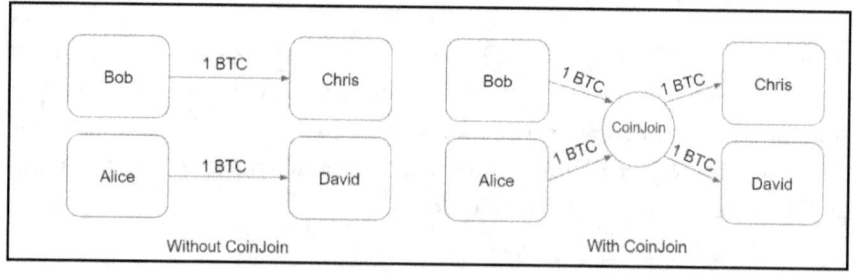

[97] (2013, August 22). CoinJoin: Bitcoin privacy for the real world – Bitcointalk. Retrieved January 20, 2021, from https://bitcointalk.org/index.php?topic=279249.0
[98] (n.d.). CoinJoin. All about cryptocurrency – BitcoinWiki. Retrieved November 16, 2020, from https://en.bitcoinwiki.org/wiki/CoinJoin

PayJoin

CoinJoin does not have to be limited to one-way transactions—two parties can pay each other through a special CoinJoin transaction known as PayJoin, which has different and perhaps better privacy features. This is because PayJoin transactions would not have specific outputs of equal value, thus it would not be as easy to spot compared to a regular CoinJoin transaction with equal outputs.[99]

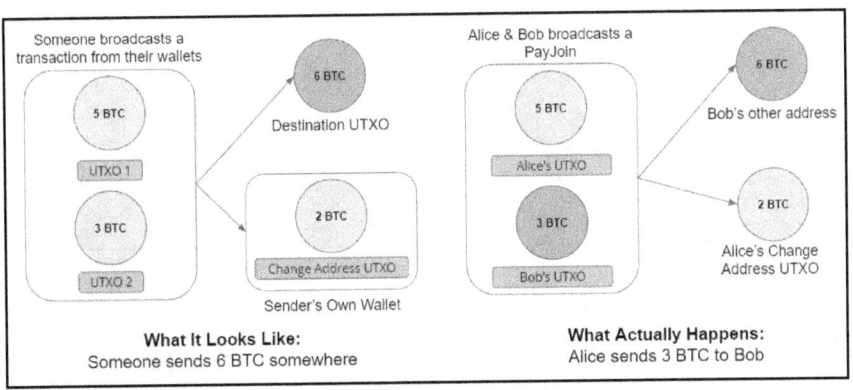

However, one issue with CoinJoin is that you will require a counterparty looking to transact with CoinJoin as well—which can be a hassle. This is where JoinMarket is useful.

JoinMarket

CoinJoin can be a hassle to use, as it only works if the right quantity is available in the right place, at the right time. Built as an improvement to the CoinJoin feature, JoinMarket helps solve this problem by creating a market for CoinJoin transactions to be executed in the most optimal way.

The way this works is by allowing CoinJoin transaction services to be supplied and demanded by two main participants—market makers and market takers. Market makers refer to CoinJoin participants who want to earn fees for allowing others to create CoinJoin transactions with them. On the other hand, market takers are CoinJoin participants who want to make

---

[99] (2020, September 4). PayJoin – Bitcoin Wiki. Retrieved November 16, 2020, from https://en.bitcoin.it/wiki/PayJoin

transactions as soon as possible, paying fees to the market makers for this privilege.

JoinMarket Orderbook

60 orders found by 26 counterparties

Type	Counterparty	Order ID	Fee	Miner Contribution/BTC	Minimum Size/BTC	Maximum Size/BTC
Absolute Fee	J521DTShAQ1zduMj	0	0.00000010	0.00000000	0.00100000	7.52563942
Absolute Fee	J5EQgLL4ne41bSaX	1	0.00000410	0.00000100	0.00027300	0.67324590
Absolute Fee	J53IBNeVtxWAwcVV	1	0.00000040	0.00000010	0.00100000	2.60698010
Absolute Fee	J55eTiKmhUDV8ovm	0	0.00000113	0.00000030	0.00100000	1.90763014
Absolute Fee	J52Srez1wpuyYHzS	0	0.00000020	0.00000005	0.00100000	2.87215618
Absolute Fee	J57EUia1gtyJggVa	0	0.00002010	0.00000500	0.15000000	0.26999999
Absolute Fee	J59ILhwZgFLhp5tH	1	0.00000060	0.00000010	0.09000000	0.99999999

Example of JoinMarket Orderbook

JoinMarkets makes use of multiple application scripts for different specific purposes. The "Yield Generator" script collects income for market makers while the "Send Payment" script acts as a market taker. The "Tumbler" script enhances privacy by automatically creating CoinJoins at random.[100]

With the creation of JoinMarkets, users can now send up to 200 BTC worth in equal-amount transactions at any time. Imagine how difficult it would have been to find that many participants at the same time to join you in making a transaction of that size, if JoinMarkets did not exist.

Taproot

Bitcoins are essentially stored in "scripts" which are within a transaction and dictate how the coins could be spent in future transactions through certain conditions.[101] When the recipient chooses to spend the funds, they must reveal the entire script and its solution. Through this method, anyone can verify that the supplied script was indeed the original script and that the specified conditions were met.

---

[100] (2020, June 17). JoinMarket – Bitcoin Wiki. Retrieved November 16, 2020, from https://en.bitcoin.it/wiki/JoinMarket

[101] (2019, January 24). Taproot Is Coming: What It Is, and How It Will Benefit Bitcoin. Retrieved November 16, 2020, from https://bitcoinmagazine.com/articles/taproot-coming-what-it-and-how-it-will-benefit-bitcoin

However, the current flaw here is that users have to reveal all existing conditions—even those that have not been met. This leads to two major complications: the amount of revealed conditions would constitute a lot of data and therefore represents a risk to privacy.

A proposed solution came in the form of the Merkelized Abstract Syntax Tree (MAST). Through this process, each spending condition is hashed separately and included in a Merkle tree to produce one single hash called the Merkle root, which locks up the funds. The value here is that if any of the Merkle tree data is revealed, only the Merkle root and Merkle path is required to verify that the particular data is really there, while the rest of the Merkle tree stays hidden. In short, only the fulfilled condition has to be revealed with MAST.[102]

The Taproot soft-fork was inspired by MAST and its possibilities, where it always includes a condition for all participants to cooperate and spend their funds. Combined with the usage of Schnorr signatures in the Bitcoin protocol, the group can remain concealed as a single entity. Schnorr signatures allow multi-signature and single-signature transactions to remain identical on the blockchain, masking them from observers.

Using the Schnorr signature algorithm, joint owners of multi-signature wallets can produce a cumulative public key and then sign it together with one signature, compared to individually publishing each key and signature for a particular transaction.[103]

---

[102] (2019, September 18). What are Taproot, MAST and Schnorr Signatures? | by Tara ....
Retrieved November 16, 2020, from https://medium.com/@tara.annison/what-are-taproot-mast-and-schnorr-signatures-b737dae20681

[103] (n.d.). Taproot & Schnorr: Scalability and Privacy Upgrades for Bitcoin. Retrieved November 16, 2020, from https://medium.com/galaxy-digital-research/taproot-schnorr-scalability-and-privacy-upgrades-for-bitcoin-e81b0df9101b

Assume **G** = *publicly known curve point,*
　　k = *private key (integer)*
　　m = *message hash (integer)*

Then the public key is **P**, where:

P = k*G

Assume **z** is a random integer, then the curve point **R** is:

R = z*G

An integer, s, is calculated as follows:

s = z + Hash (r $|$ $|$ P $|$ $|$ m) * k

Where: **r** = *x-coordinate of curve point R,*
　　$|$ $|$ = *binary concatenation*

Signature = (r, s), *where both r and s are integers.*

Signature creation algorithm of Schnorr Signatures

Taproot promises to increase Bitcoin's fungibility, improve the functionality of smart contracts, and boost privacy by making all transactions appear the same to blockchain observers.[104] Besides that, the aggregation of multiple private keys into one "master key" to perform transactions may potentially reduce transaction fees and lower node operations costs, both vital for the long-term scalability of the network.

Note that as of December 2020, the Taproot upgrade has not yet been deployed. Until then, Taproot functionalities will not be usable.

---

[104] (2020, September 29). The Bitcoin Schnorr / Taproot upgrade explained » Brave New Coin. Retrieved November 16, 2020, from https://bravenewcoin.com/insights/the-3-most-promising-bitcoin-improvement-proposals-bips

What's Next?

Despite being 12 years old as of time of writing, Bitcoin still has endless room to grow, subject to operational and security limitations. One can expect to see many more proposals, improvements, and ideas being worked on Bitcoin in the coming months and years.

Initiatives that promise to improve scalability and privacy features on Bitcoin will most likely continue to be the main focus for the Bitcoin developers in making it a truly viable global payments system.

CHAPTER 9: BEYOND BITCOIN

The world of blockchain technology and cryptocurrency goes beyond bitcoin. There are now many different cryptocurrencies that run on various blockchains and have a multitude of functions. These coins are commonly referred to as alternative coins to bitcoin or 'altcoins'. In this chapter, we will be looking at some of the largest and most popular cryptocurrencies in use today.

As we have seen previously, Bitcoin has many challenges to overcome before it can be universally adopted as a legitimate form of currency. However, other cryptocurrencies are also racing against them to reach a similar goal, by attempting to solve the problems that Bitcoin has posed. While other platforms and cryptocurrencies may adopt high-risk, light-speed approaches to development, Bitcoin's progress is relatively slower and more stable, in an attempt to mitigate the risk of things breaking within the platform.

Bitcoin Forks

Bitcoin forks occur when there are changes made to the current protocol and are usually conducted to add new features. It is also used to undo any devastating hacks or bugs. In these cases, a consensus is required before the changes are implemented. Otherwise, the blockchain may be permanently split, resulting in the birth of new blockchains such as Bitcoin Cash and Bitcoin SV.

Bitcoin Cash

Although it has 'bitcoin' in its name, Bitcoin Cash is a different cryptocurrency and should not be mistaken for bitcoin. Bitcoin Cash was created when some developers wanted to increase the amount of transactions in a block by increasing the block size to 32MB, thereby effectively speeding up transactions by almost 21 times and lowering costs.

To implement this change, a hard fork was initiated in 2017, splitting the bitcoin blockchain into the original and new Bitcoin Cash network. After the fork, users who had some bitcoin before the block would also end up having an equal amount of Bitcoin Cash.

Although there are only a few key differences between Bitcoin Cash and the original bitcoin, the prices of both assets tell a different story. Bitcoin Cash has a much lower value compared to bitcoin. Although users may be more tempted to use Bitcoin Cash, it has become very centralized in the hands of a few mining pools, which goes against bitcoin's decentralization ideals. Paired with the existing popularity and utility of bitcoin, it is even more difficult for Bitcoin Cash to truly dethrone its predecessor. Additionally, the team behind Bitcoin Cash has been identified whereas Bitcoin's creators remain anonymous.

On 15th November 2020, Bitcoin Cash underwent another fork, caused by a dispute between two camps of the Bitcoin Cash community, namely Bitcoin Cash ABC (BCH ABC) and Bitcoin Cash Node (BCHN). The rift began when a group of developers which makes up BCH ABC proposed an update to charge 8% tax on profits earned by miners to finance the future development of Bitcoin Cash. This was heavily opposed by the Bitcoin Cash Node community. With heavy support from miners, Bitcoin Cash Node inherited the BCH ticker while BCH ABC diverged away into a separate blockchain.

Bitcoin SV

Bitcoin Cash ABC and Bitcoin Cash Node was not the first hard fork within the Bitcoin Cash community. The first hard fork of Bitcoin Cash was in November 2018, splitting the network into the original Bitcoin Cash and the new Bitcoin SV blockchain, which was created to strictly follow Satoshi

186

Nakamoto's original vision for Bitcoin. A major difference between the two networks is block size. While Bitcoin Cash can handle up to 32MB of transactions per block, Bitcoin SV quadruples that amount, boasting a block size limit of up to 128MB.

However, the developers were far from done. On 24 July 2019, Bitcoin SV received the 'Quasar' protocol upgrade, which increased the block size limit from 128MB to 2GB. However, miners have signalled their intention to set a lower hard cap at 512MB, which is still much larger compared to its predecessors.

A few weeks after the implementation, miners struggled to process a 210MB block of transactions, which prevented them from relaying transactions to the network.[105]

Smart Contract Platforms

Smart contracts are programs which can be written to perform highly specific and sophisticated actions when certain conditions are fulfilled. Although the Bitcoin protocol facilitates a "weak" implementation of smart contracts, it is difficult to expand upon the idea due scripting language limitations that Bitcoin uses.[106] This is where platforms like Ethereum and Polkadot step in to fill the gaps to produce more advanced smart contracts for a myriad of applications such as finance, healthcare, and entertainment.

Ethereum

Ethereum is a decentralized platform for making digital payments, or pretty much a world computer—accessible from anyone and anywhere. It is also the second-largest cryptocurrency by market capitalization behind Bitcoin.

The Ethereum blockchain makes use of its own native currency called ether, which is generated by mining, similar to how bitcoins are created. However, the similarities end there as Ethereum is capable of so much

---

[105] (2019, August 10). In Big Block Hard Fork, Craig Wright's Bitcoin Has Left Nodes ....
Retrieved November 18, 2020, from https://www.coindesk.com/in-big-block-hard-fork-craig-wrights-bitcoin-has-left-nodes-behind

[106] (n.d.). Ethereum Whitepaper | ethereum.org. Retrieved November 18, 2020, from https://ethereum.org/en/whitepaper/

more as it allows the users on the network to publish and interact with smart contracts. Smart contracts have become the basis of many decentralized applications (dApps) that currently operate on the Ethereum network.

Ethereum's protocol allows for different projects and tokens to be launched on the network. Since the launch of Ethereum, many other tokens have been launched on top of the Ethereum network by complying with certain standards. These standards, such as ERC-20 and ERC-721 have been established to allow these tokens to operate seamlessly within the Ethereum ecosystem.

The ERC-20 token standard is used to create fungible tokens that have been adopted by many cryptocurrency projects. These tokens are interchangeable and can be freely exchanged with each other.

The ERC-721 token standard, on the other hand, is used to create non-fungible tokens (NFT). These tokens are used to represent unique or one-of-a-kind assets that have different characteristics and values. Non-fungible tokens have been used as limited edition digital art, collectible cards, and many more.

You can easily purchase ether through most cryptocurrency exchanges. Although Ethereum mining is an option, it has become industrialized over the years and may not be recommended for individuals.

Polkadot

Polkadot is a blockchain protocol designed to support multiple purpose-built blockchains under one unified network. A brief rundown on some of the main issues that Polkadot aims to tackle:

1. **Scale** – With multiple interoperable blockchains built on top of it, transactions can be processed in parallel across different chains while maintaining connectivity, greatly increasing throughput and scalability.

2. **Specialization** – Blockchain protocols are typically built for specific use cases, and it can be very difficult to have a one-size-fits- all solution (think Bitcoin not being able to handle smart contracts too

188

well, or Ethereum struggling to handle Cryptokitties at its peak). On Polkadot, each blockchain—also called "parachains"—can be optimized for specific use cases such as file storage and transaction processing, for maximum efficiency.

3. **Governance** – Having separate blockchains also means that each parachain can self-govern and upgrade their protocol as required without affecting the rest of the network. This potentially allows for quicker iterations, fixes or changes compared to existing single-blockchain networks.

Polkadot's infrastructure begins with the relay chain, which acts as the central chain. Each chain that runs on Polkadot is called a parachain as they run parallel to the main relay chain, and is built on top of the relay chain.[107]

Besides blockchains built on top of Polkadot's own relay chain, it is also interoperable with blockchains that have vastly different technology stacks such as Ethereum and Bitcoin through bridges.

Stablecoins

Stablecoins are a form of cryptocurrency that aims to have its value pegged to a national currency such as the US dollar or a commodity such as gold. US dollar stablecoins are the most popular form of stablecoins and have gained popularity in recent years.

US dollar stablecoins provide traders with the ability to have a stable portfolio pegged to the US dollar instead of a volatile portfolio held in bitcoin. Tether and Dai are some of the more widely used stablecoins.

Tether

Originally known as Realcoin in 2014, Tether is the undisputed leader of stablecoins. Tether is meant to represent the value of the US dollar, where 1 unit of Tether is equivalent to 1 US dollar. Tether has mostly maintained a stable value throughout its history pegged to the US dollar.

---

[107] (2020, September 24). What Is Polkadot? Introduction to DOT | Crypto Briefing. Retrieved November 18, 2020, from https://cryptobriefing.com/what-is-polkadot-introduction-dot/

On 6 October 2014, the first Tether stablecoins were issued on the Bitcoin network using the Omni Layer protocol. In order to uphold its peg to the US dollar, Tether claims that each token is backed by an equivalent amount of US dollar in its bank reserves.

However, Tether is not without controversy. There have been allegations that Tether is no longer fully backed by bank reserves and that a portion of its reserves includes affiliate company loans.[108]

Despite the controversies, as the first stablecoin, Tether is still extremely popular with traders. It is listed on almost all cryptocurrency exchanges as a trading pair against cryptocurrencies. Its popularity has seen it become one of the top 3 largest cryptocurrencies by market capitalization.

Dai

Contrary to Tether, Dai is not backed by fiat currencies but is instead backed by cryptocurrencies. Dai is a form of debt that is taken out based on the amount of underlying assets deposited as collateral.[109]

Dai functions as one of the major stablecoins used on the Ethereum platform, where its peg is maintained due to over-collateralization of cryptocurrency assets. In other words, to get $1 worth of Dai, users have to deposit at least $1.50 in ether or other cryptocurrencies.[110]

The current version of DAI, also known as multi-collateral Dai, is an updated iteration that supports multiple cryptocurrency assets as collateral to create Dai. The previous version, now known as Sai is called single-collateral Dai because it can only be generated using ether as collateral.

---

[108] (2019, March 14). Tether's US Dollar Peg Is No Longer Credible – Forbes. Retrieved November 18, 2020, from https://www.forbes.com/sites/francescoppola/2019/03/14/tethers-u-s-dollar-peg-is-no-longer-credible/

[109] (n.d.). Whitepaper – Maker DAO. Retrieved November 18, 2020, from https://makerdao.com/whitepaper/

[110] (2019, April 26). DAI Struggles to Maintain $1 Peg, But MakerDAO Supporters Still Believe. Retrieved November 18, 2020, from https://cointelegraph.com/news/dai-has-been-struggling-to-maintain-its-1-peg-but-the-makerdao-community-believes-it-will-soon-be-cryptos-default-stablecoin

Privacy Coins

Many people think that Bitcoin transactions are totally anonymous and are not traceable. However, this is not entirely true. Bitcoin promises some pseudonymity where some information is private and protected, but not all of it.

Anyone with the proper technical know-how and understanding of the Bitcoin protocol can track down transactions with some effort. This is where privacy coins are favored, as they allow users to achieve a higher degree of anonymity when making transactions through a blockchain.

Dash

Widely considered as the first privacy coin to be created, Dash was a fork of the original Bitcoin code but with an interesting twist—an optional form of privacy through their own modified version of CoinJoin called PrivateSend.[111] PrivateSend masks various transactions by mixing them together and it is then verified on the blockchain as one single transaction.

Monero

One of the top privacy coins in use today, Monero is built to be private by default, making use of stealth addresses and ring confidential transactions (RingCT). Stealth addresses are single-use addresses that are created for each transaction by a sender.

Payments sent from the original address are routed through these stealth addresses to prevent any linkability to the recipient that can be observed on the blockchain. However, this poses another challenge, as it is not entirely private if the senders can trace a recipient's set of transactions based on the amount sent to them. Therefore, ring signatures are used to mask the output amounts so that total untraceability is ensured.

---

[111] (n.d.). Privatesend – Dash Core. Retrieved November 18, 2020, from https://dashcore.readme.io/docs/core-guide-dash-features-privatesend

CLOSING REMARKS

First of all, give yourself a good pat on the back! If you are reading this, it means that you are now up-to-date with Bitcoin, one of the most fascinating forms of money the world has ever seen.

Thank you for your time and we hope you have enjoyed reading the *How to Bitcoin* book as much as we had fun writing it. The cryptocurrency rabbit hole is deep and we have just only scratched the surface here. We hope that you will be inspired to join us on this journey.

If you would like to learn more about what comes next after sound digital money, check out another one of our publications on Decentralized Finance (DeFi). Our ***How to DeFi*** book will give you further insights on what the future of finance will look like.

Welcome to the world of cryptocurrencies!

APPENDIX

CoinGecko's Recommended Bitcoin Resources

Reads
Grubles – https://notgrubles.medium.com/
Jameson Lopp's Bitcoin Resources – https://www.lopp.net/bitcoin-information.html
Jameson Lopp's Lightning Network Resources – https://www.lopp.net/lightning-information.html/
Jimmy Song – https://jimmysong.medium.com/
Pierre Rochard – https://www.pierrerochard.com/
Unchained Capital – https://unchained-capital.com/blog/

Newsletters
Bitcoin Optech – https://bitcoinops.org/

Podcast
Stephen Livera – https://stephanlivera.com/
Unscrypted Podcast – https://aantonop.com/category/podcasts/unscrypted-pod/
What Bitcoin Did – https://www.whatbitcoindid.com/
Lightning Junkies – https://lightningjunkies.net/

Videos

Bitcoin Beginner's Important Videos –
https://www.youtube.com/playlist?list=PLeEqJMaPXEpryW67EIvIDs
0UzHA_cyL-V

Andreas Antanapolous – https://www.youtube.com/c/aantonop/videos

Robert Breedlove – https://www.youtube.com/c/RobertBreedlove22

Other Books We Recommend

Mastering Bitcoin – https://www.goodreads.com/book/show/21820378-mastering-bitcoin

The Bitcoin Standard –
https://www.goodreads.com/book/show/36448501-the-bitcoin-standard

Thank God for Bitcoin –
https://www.goodreads.com/book/show/56049234-thank-god-for-bitcoin

References
Chapter 1: Bitcoin and Money

(2008, April 27). Moody's - Credit Rating - Mortgages - The New York Times. Retrieved November 12, 2020, from https://www.nytimes.com/2008/04/27/magazine/27Credit-t.html

(2013, March 13). President Nixon: The Man Who Sold the World Fiat Money .... Retrieved November 10, 2020, from https://blogs.cfainstitute.org/investor/2013/03/13/president-nixon-the-man-who-sold-the-world-fiat-money/

(2013, September 10). Inside Bitcoin, The Programmable Currency For Our Digital .... Retrieved November 18, 2020, from https://techcrunch.com/2013/09/10/disrupt-sf-13-bitcoin-panel/

(2013, September 10). Inside Bitcoin, The Programmable Currency For Our Digital .... Retrieved November 18, 2020, from https://techcrunch.com/2013/09/10/disrupt-sf-13-bitcoin-panel/

(2016, November 8). Rupee notes in India: Narendra Modi just banned Rs500 and .... Retrieved November 26, 2020, from https://qz.com/india/830774/rupee-notes-in-india-narendra-modi-just-banned-rs500-and-rs1000-notes-to-fight-corruption-and-terrorism/

(2018, December 15). Who Controls Bitcoin Core? – Cypherpunk Cogitations. Retrieved November 24, 2020, from https://blog.lopp.net/who-controls-bitcoin-core-/

(2018, August 21). PayPal Account Limitations: what they are and what you can .... Retrieved November 17, 2020, from https://www.paypal.com/us/brc/article/understanding-account-limitations

(2019, August 1). A History Guide to the 2008 Financial Crisis: What Caused the .... Retrieved November 12, 2020, from https://www.historyextra.com/period/modern/financial-crisis-crash-explained-facts-causes/

(2020, January 27). Growth In The Level Of Precision Of Bitcoin ... – BitMEX Blog. Retrieved November 24, 2020, from https://blog.bitmex.com/bitcoin-transaction-output-value-precision/

(2020, April 26). What Actually is Programmable Money? – LinkedIn. Retrieved November 18, 2020, from https://www.linkedin.com/pulse/what-actually-programmable-money-antony-lewis

(2010, May 18). Pizza for bitcoins? – Bitcoin Forum. Retrieved January 20, 2021, from https://bitcointalk.org/index.php?topic=137.0

(2020, July 6). Hong Kong security law: Police handed power to do .... Retrieved November 10, 2020, from https://hongkongfp.com/2020/07/06/breaking-hong-kong-security-law-police-handed-power-to-do-warrantless-searches-freeze-assets-intercept-comms-control-internet/

(2020, July 27). 1913 Federal Reserve Act Definition – Investopedia. Retrieved November 10, 2020, from https://www.investopedia.com/terms/f/1913-federal-reserve-act.asp

(2020, August 27). Cryptocurrency usage in Venezuela – Chainalysis blog. Retrieved November 20, 2020, from https://blog.chainalysis.com/reports/venezuela-cryptocurrency-market-2020

(2020, October 9). Iran sanctions: US moves to isolate 'major' banks – BBC News. Retrieved January 20, 2021, from https://www.bbc.com/news/world-middle-east-54476894

(n.d.). Bitcoin P2P e-cash paper – Cryptography mailing list. Retrieved November 10, 2020, from https://www.metzdowd.com/pipermail/cryptography/2008-October/014810.html

(n.d.). Bitcoin / Blocks — Blockchair. Retrieved November 12, 2020, from https://blockchair.com/bitcoin/blocks

(n.d.). Address: 1A1zP1eP5QGefi2DMPTfTL5SLmv7DivfNa .... Retrieved November 12, 2020, from https://www.blockchain.com/btc/address/1A1zP1eP5QGefi2DMPTfTL5SLmv7DivfNa

(n.d.). What is Bitcoin? Price in USD, Mining, Bitcoin ... – Bitcoin Wiki. Retrieved November 10, 2020, from https://en.bitcoinwiki.org/wiki/Bitcoin

(n.d.). Profit distribution and loss coverage rules for central banks. Retrieved November 10, 2020, from https://www.ecb.europa.eu/pub/pdf/scpops/ecbop169.en.pdf

(n.d.). bitcoin/COPYING at master · bitcoin/bitcoin · GitHub. Retrieved November 10, 2020, from https://github.com/bitcoin/bitcoin/blob/master/COPYING

(n.d.). What is open source software? | Opensource.com. Retrieved November 10, 2020, from https://opensource.com/resources/what-open-source

(n.d.). Inflación de 2018 cerró en 1.698.488%, según la Asamblea .... Retrieved November 26, 2020, from https://efectococuyo.com/economia/inflacion-de-2018-cerro-en-1-698-488-segun-la-asamblea-nacional/

(n.d.). Why Bitcoin Is Not a Viable Currency Option – Knowledge .... Retrieved November 24, 2020, from https://kw.wharton.upenn.edu/kwfellows/files/2018/06/2018-08-30-Bitcoin-Student-Series.pdf

(n.d.). Inflation Calculator. Retrieved January 20, 2021, from https://www.usinflationcalculator.com/

Chapter 2: Anatomy of Bitcoin

Antonopoulos, Andreas M. (2017). *The Internet of Money*. Merkle Bloom.

(2020, June 30). UTXO Definition – Investopedia. Retrieved November 27, 2020, from https://www.investopedia.com/terms/u/utxo.asp

(n.d.). Unspent Transaction Output (UTXO) | Binance Academy. Retrieved November 27, 2020, from https://academy.binance.com/en/glossary/unspent-transaction-output-utxo

(n.d.). Vocabulary – Bitcoin.org. Retrieved January 20, 2021, from https://bitcoin.org/en/vocabulary

(n.d.). 8. Mining and Consensus – Mastering Bitcoin [Book] – O'Reilly. Retrieved January 20, 2021, from https://www.oreilly.com/library/view/mastering-bitcoin/9781491902639/ch08.html

(n.d.). Double-Spending – Corporate Finance Institute. Retrieved January 20, 2021, from https://corporatefinanceinstitute.com/resources/knowledge/other/double-spending/

Chapter 3: The History of Bitcoin

(2010, August 16). Strange block 74638 – Bitcoin Forum. Retrieved November 10, 2020, from https://bitcointalk.org/index.php?topic=822.0

(2011, June 19). Bitcoin prices plummet on hacked exchange | Ars Technica. Retrieved December 4, 2020, from https://arstechnica.com/tech-policy/2011/06/bitcoin-price-plummets-on-compromised-exchange/

(2011, June 19). Bitcoin collapses on malicious trade • The Register. Retrieved December 18, 2020, from https://www.theregister.com/2011/06/19/bitcoin_values_collapse_again/

(2013, June 27). The DEA Seized Bitcoins In A Silk Road Drug Raid .... Retrieved December 4, 2020, from https://techcrunch.com/2013/06/27/the-dea-seized-bitcoins-in-a-silk-road-drug-raid/

(2016, July 22). Value overflow incident – Bitcoin Wiki. Retrieved November 10, 2020, from https://en.bitcoin.it/wiki/Value_overflow_incident

(2017, June 20). Bitcoin Miners Are Signaling Support for the New York .... Retrieved January 19, 2021, from https://bitcoinmagazine.com/articles/miners-are-signaling-support-new-york-agreement-heres-what-means

(2017, June 27). The Risks of Segregated Witness: Possible Problems Under .... Retrieved November 10, 2020, from https://www.coindesk.com/the-risks-of-bitcoins-segregated-witness-problems-under-us-contract-law

(2018, June 20). The Mt. Gox Hack— What's in your Bitcoin Wallet? –
Medium. Retrieved December 4, 2020, from
https://medium.com/dataseries/the-rise-and-fall-of-mt-gox-whats-in-
your-bitcoin-wallet-bd5eb4106f4e

(2019, January 11). Bitcoin's Biggest Hack In History: 184.4 Billion Bitcoin
from …. Retrieved January 20, 2021, from
https://hackernoon.com/bitcoins-biggest-hack-in-history-184-4-
ded46310d4ef

(n.d.). Bitcoin halving 2020: research and data for … – CoinDesk. Retrieved
November 10, 2020, from https://www.coindesk.com/crypto-
investment-research/bitcoin-halving-2020-research-report

(n.d.). Bitcoin Halving Countdown – CoinGecko. Retrieved November 25,
2020, from https://www.coingecko.com/en/explain/bitcoin_halving

(n.d.) What Is Lightning Network And How It Works – Cointelegraph.
Retrieved November 17, 2020, from
https://cointelegraph.com/lightning-network-101/what-is-lightning-
network-and-how-it-works

(n.d.). 99.98% – Bitcoin Uptime Tracker (Updated Live). Retrieved
November 26, 2020, from
https://www.buybitcoinworldwide.com/bitcoin-uptime/

(n.d.). bips/bip-0050.mediawiki at master · bitcoin/bips · GitHub.
Retrieved November 10, 2020, from
https://github.com/bitcoin/bips/blob/master/bip-0050.mediawiki

(n.d.). Bitcoin Obituaries - Bitcoin Declared Dead 350+ … – 99Bitcoins.
Retrieved January 20, 2021, from https://99bitcoins.com/bitcoin-
obituaries/

Chapter 4: Keeping your Bitcoin Safe

(2018, October 22). How to get an address from a private key on Bitcoin – Crypto .... Retrieved January 20, 2021, from https://www.crypto-lyon.fr/how-to-get-an-address-from-a-private-key-on-bitcoin.html

(2020, January 22). Bitcoin address formats and performance ... – FixedFloat. Retrieved November 25, 2020, from https://fixedfloat.com/blog/guides/bitcoin-address-formats

(2020, February 10). Mt. Gox: The Story Of The Biggest Ever Bitcoin Hack | Trading .... Retrieved January 20, 2021, from https://trading-education.com/mt-gox-the-story-of-the-biggest-ever-bitcoin-hack

(2020, June 23). IP Address Definition – Investopedia. Retrieved January 20, 2021, from https://www.investopedia.com/terms/i/ip-address.asp

(2020, September 7). Exodus Wallet Review: What is Exodus? Is ... – BitDegree. Retrieved November 20, 2020, from https://www.bitdegree.org/crypto/exodus-wallet-review

(2020, October 13). Bech32 – Bitcoin Wiki. Retrieved November 25, 2020, from https://en.bitcoin.it/wiki/Bech32

(2020, October 15). What is two-factor authentication (2FA) and how does ... – Norton. Retrieved November 26, 2020, from https://us.norton.com/internetsecurity-how-to-importance-two-factor-authentication.html

(n.d.). 4. Keys, Addresses - Mastering Bitcoin, 2nd Edition ... – O'Reilly. Retrieved December 16, 2020, from https://www.oreilly.com/library/view/mastering-bitcoin-2nd/9781491954379/ch04.html

(n.d.). The Universe By Numbers – The Physics of the Universe. Retrieved January 20, 2021, from https://www.physicsoftheuniverse.com/numbers.html

(n.d.). Bitcoin blockchain size 2009-2021 | Statista. Retrieved January 20, 2021, from https://www.statista.com/statistics/647523/worldwide-bitcoin-blockchain-size/

(n.d.). Does Atomic Wallet have fees to send or receive the assets .... Retrieved November 20, 2020, from https://support.atomicwallet.io/article/77-does-atomic-wallet-have-fees-to-send-or-receive-the-assets

(n.d.). Stealth Mode – Samourai Wallet. Retrieved November 22, 2020, from https://samouraiwallet.com/stealth

(n.d.). Coinbase pricing and fees disclosures | Coinbase Help. Retrieved November 22, 2020, from https://help.coinbase.com/en/coinbase/trading-and-funding/pricing-and-fees/fees

(n.d.). Trezor White – Official Trezor Shop. Retrieved November 23, 2020, from https://shop.trezor.io/product/trezor-one-white

(n.d.). Trezor Model T – Official Trezor Shop. Retrieved November 23, 2020, from https://shop.trezor.io/product/trezor-model-t

(n.d.). Phishing | What Is Phishing? – Phishing.org. Retrieved January 20, 2021, from https://www.phishing.org/what-is-phishing

Chapter 5: Getting your First Bitcoin
(2020, September 16). Kraken Becomes First Crypto Exchange to Become a US Bank .... Retrieved November 23, 2020, from https://www.nasdaq.com/articles/kraken-becomes-first-crypto-exchange-to-become-a-us-bank-2020-09-16

(n.d.). LocalBitcoins Review: Is LocalBitcoins Safe ... – CoinSutra. Retrieved November 10, 2020, from https://coinsutra.com/localbitcoins-review/

Chapter 6: Storing your Bitcoin Safely

(2020, January 22). Shamir Backup – Trezor Wiki. Retrieved January 20, 2021, from https://wiki.trezor.io/Shamir_Backup

(2020, October 9). [Lightning-dev] Partial LND Vulnerability Disclosure, Upgrade .... Retrieved January 20, 2021, from https://lists.linuxfoundation.org/pipermail/lightning-dev/2020-October/002819.html

(n.d.). Official Trezor Shop | Trezor Black – Trezor Model T. Retrieved November 16, 2020, from https://shop.trezor.io/product/trezor-one-black

(n.d.). ACINQ | A Bitcoin Technology Company. Retrieved December 17, 2020, from https://acinq.co/

(n.d.). What is two-factor authentication (2FA) and how does ... – Norton. Retrieved January 20, 2021, from https://us.norton.com/internetsecurity-how-to-importance-two-factor-authentication.html

Chapter 7: Advanced Bitcoin Wallets

(2017, June 20). Bitcoin Miners Are Signaling Support for the New York .... Retrieved January 19, 2021, from https://bitcoinmagazine.com/articles/miners-are-signaling-support-new-york-agreement-heres-what-means

(2019, March 11). Samourai Wallet — Collaborative Transactions – "Cahoots". Retrieved January 20, 2021, from https://blog.samouraiwallet.com/post/183378923792/collaborative-transactions-cahoots

(2019, October 24). Why Run a Node? – Casa Blog. Retrieved January 20, 2021, from https://blog.keys.casa/why-run-a-node/

(2020, June 15). Dealing with Coinjoin Change Outputs – Bitcoin Q+A. Retrieved January 20, 2021, from https://www.bitcoinqna.com/post/dealing-with-coinjoin-change-outputs

(n.d.). Running A Full Node – Bitcoin.org. Retrieved January 20, 2021, from https://bitcoin.org/en/full-node

(n.d.). About – Bitcoin Core. Retrieved January 20, 2021, from https://bitcoincore.org/en/about/

(n.d.). Releases · bitcoin/bitcoin · GitHub. Retrieved January 20, 2021, from https://github.com/bitcoin/bitcoin/releases

(n.d.). Digital signature – Wikipedia. Retrieved January 20, 2021, from https://en.wikipedia.org/wiki/Digital_signature

(n.d.). P2P Network – Bitcoin.org. Retrieved January 20, 2021, from https://developer.bitcoin.org/devguide/p2p_network.html

(n.d.). Bitnodes. Retrieved January 20, 2021, from https://bitnodes.io/

(n.d.). Fee Estimates – Statoshi. Retrieved January 20, 2021, from https://statoshi.info/dashboard/db/fee-estimates

(n.d.). Basic commands to interact with the Bitcoin Core RPC console. Retrieved January 20, 2021, from https://medium.com/@peterjd42/basic-commands-to-interact-with-the-bitcoin-core-rpc-console-180da2c2dc45

(n.d.). Feature Comparison – Samourai Wallet. Retrieved December 17, 2020, from https://samouraiwallet.com/features/comparison

(n.d.). Samourai Wallet – Features. Retrieved December 17, 2020, from https://samouraiwallet.com/features

(n.d.). Bitcoin Q&A: Samourai, Wasabi, and privacy on Huffduffer. Retrieved December 17, 2020, from https://huffduffer.com/uwefassnacht/544981

(n.d.). STONEWALL – Samourai Wallet. Retrieved December 17, 2020, from https://samouraiwallet.com/stonewall

(n.d.). Whirlpool – Samourai Wallet. Retrieved December 17, 2020, from https://samouraiwallet.com/whirlpool

(n.d.). Download – Samourai Wallet. Retrieved December 17, 2020, from https://samouraiwallet.com/download

(n.d.). Tor (anonymity network) – Wikipedia. Retrieved January 20, 2021, from https://en.wikipedia.org/wiki/Tor_(anonymity_network)

(n.d.). Doxing – Wikipedia. Retrieved January 20, 2021, from https://en.wikipedia.org/wiki/Doxing

(n.d.) What Is Lightning Network And How It Works – Cointelegraph. Retrieved November 17, 2020, from https://cointelegraph.com/lightning-network-101/what-is-lightning-network-and-how-it-works

Chapter 8: Bitcoin's Improvements

(2013, August 22). CoinJoin: Bitcoin privacy for the real world – Bitcointalk. Retrieved January 20, 2021, from https://bitcointalk.org/index.php?topic=279249.0

(2018, June 30). Discreet Log Contracts: invisible smart contracts on the Bitcoin .... Retrieved November 16, 2020, from https://medium.com/@gertjaap/discreet-log-contracts-invisible-smart-contracts-on-the-bitcoin-blockchain-cc8afbdbf0db

(2019, January 24). Taproot Is Coming: What It Is, and How It Will Benefit Bitcoin. Retrieved November 16, 2020, from https://bitcoinmagazine.com/articles/taproot-coming-what-it-and-how-it-will-benefit-bitcoin

(2019, February 5). Bitcoin's 'Lightning Torch' Explained: What It Is and ... – CoinDesk. Retrieved January 20, 2021, from https://www.coindesk.com/bitcoins-lightning-torch-has-blazed-through-37-countries-so-far

(2019, March 14). Tether's US Dollar Peg Is No Longer Credible – Forbes. Retrieved November 18, 2020, from https://www.forbes.com/sites/francescoppola/2019/03/14/tethers-u-s-dollar-peg-is-no-longer-credible/

(2019, April 26). DAI Struggles to Maintain $1 Peg, But MakerDAO Supporters Still Believe. Retrieved November 18, 2020, from https://cointelegraph.com/news/dai-has-been-struggling-to-maintain-its-1-peg-but-the-makerdao-community-believes-it-will-soon-be-cryptos-default-stablecoin

(2019, August 10). In Big Block Hard Fork, Craig Wright's Bitcoin Has Left Nodes .... Retrieved November 18, 2020, from https://www.coindesk.com/in-big-block-hard-fork-craig-wrights-bitcoin-has-left-nodes-behind

(2019, September 18). What are Taproot, MAST and Schnorr Signatures? | by Tara .... Retrieved November 16, 2020, from https://medium.com/@tara.annison/what-are-taproot-mast-and-schnorr-signatures-b737dae20681

(2020, April 21). What are Discreet Log Contracts in Crypto? – HedgeTrade Blog. Retrieved November 16, 2020, from https://hedgetrade.com/discreet-log-contracts/

(2020, June 11). Re: [bitcoin-dev] CoinPool, exploring generic payment pools .... Retrieved November 16, 2020, from https://www.mail-archive.com/bitcoin-dev@lists.linuxfoundation.org/msg08997.html

(2020, June 17). JoinMarket – Bitcoin Wiki. Retrieved November 16, 2020, from https://en.bitcoin.it/wiki/JoinMarket

(2020, June 28). Atomic Swaps Defined – Investopedia. Retrieved November 16, 2020, from https://www.investopedia.com/terms/a/atomic-swaps.asp

(2020, June 30). UTXO Definition – Investopedia. Retrieved November 27, 2020, from https://www.investopedia.com/terms/u/utxo.asp

(2020, August 11). Payment Pools: Bitcoin's Next Layer Two Protocol? – Bitcoin .... Retrieved November 16, 2020, from https://bitcoinmagazine.com/articles/building-on-taproot-payment-pools-could-be-bitcoins-next-layer-two-protocol

(2020, August 18). Parathreads · Polkadot Wiki. Retrieved November 18, 2020, from https://wiki.polkadot.network/docs/en/learn-parathreads

(2020, August 19). CoinSwap – Bitcoin Wiki. Retrieved November 16, 2020, from https://en.bitcoin.it/wiki/CoinSwap

(2020, September 4). PayJoin – Bitcoin Wiki. Retrieved November 16, 2020, from https://en.bitcoin.it/wiki/PayJoin

(2020, September 24). What Is Polkadot? Introduction to DOT | Crypto Briefing. Retrieved November 18, 2020, from https://cryptobriefing.com/what-is-polkadot-introduction-dot/

(2020, September 29). The Bitcoin Schnorr / Taproot upgrade explained » Brave New Coin. Retrieved November 16, 2020, from https://bravenewcoin.com/insights/the-3-most-promising-bitcoin-improvement-proposals-bips

(2020, October 13). Architecture · Polkadot Wiki. Retrieved November 18, 2020, from https://wiki.polkadot.network/docs/en/learn-architecture

(2020, October 13). Bridges · Polkadot Wiki. Retrieved November 18, 2020, from https://wiki.polkadot.network/docs/en/learn-bridges

(n.d.) What Is Lightning Network And How It Works – Cointelegraph. Retrieved November 17, 2020, from https://cointelegraph.com/lightning-network-101/what-is-lightning-network-and-how-it-works.

(n.d.). CoinJoin. All about cryptocurrency – BitcoinWiki. Retrieved November 16, 2020, from https://en.bitcoinwiki.org/wiki/CoinJoin

(n.d.). Taproot & Schnorr: Scalability and Privacy Upgrades for Bitcoin. Retrieved November 16, 2020, from https://medium.com/galaxy-digital-research/taproot-schnorr-scalability-and-privacy-upgrades-for-bitcoin-e81b0df9101b

(n.d.). Ethereum Whitepaper | ethereum.org. Retrieved November 18, 2020, from https://ethereum.org/en/whitepaper/

(n.d.). Whitepaper – Maker DAO. Retrieved November 18, 2020, from https://makerdao.com/whitepaper/

(n.d.). Privatesend – Dash Core. Retrieved November 18, 2020, from https://dashcore.readme.io/docs/core-guide-dash-features-privatesend

(n.d.). Unspent Transaction Output (UTXO) | Binance Academy. Retrieved November 27, 2020, from https://academy.binance.com/en/glossary/unspent-transaction-output-utxo

(n.d.). Vocabulary – Bitcoin.org. Retrieved January 20, 2021, from https://bitcoin.org/en/vocabulary

(n.d.). Double-Spending – Corporate Finance Institute. Retrieved January 20, 2021, from https://corporatefinanceinstitute.com/resources/knowledge/other/double-spending/

GLOSSARY

Index	Term	Description
A	Altcoins	Alternative to Bitcoin—all cryptocurrencies that was launched after Bitcoin
B	Blockchain Split	A blockchain that diverged into two paths
C	Centralized exchange	A trading platform that is operated by a central party
	Consensus	A majority agreement within a group
	Cryptography	A method to secure and protect information through codes
	Custodial	Refers to a third party having control over your assets
D	Decentralized Applications (dApp)	Applications built on decentralized network, where the underlying software is open-source
	Distributed Denial-of-service (DDoS)	A cybersecurity attack that disrupts the normal traffic of a server or network

Index	Term	Description
	Derivatives	Financial contracts that derive value from the underlying asset
	Difficulty	The complexity in solving the cryptographic algorithm
F	Fiat	Currencies issued by a government
	Fork	A hard fork is the permanent divergence of a blockchain into two, while a soft fork is a backward-compatible update to a decentralized blockchain protocol
	Fungible	The property of an item which has interchangeable units. For example, a $1 note is interchangeable with another $1 note, hence it is fungible. In contrast, a place ticket assigned with a unique name and seat number is not interchangeable with another ticket, hence it is non-fungible
G	Genesis Block	The very first block of a blockchain
H	Halving	The event when the block rewards for mining is halved
	Hashpower	The power required by a computer to run and solve the mathematical hashing to successfully mine a block
	Hashing Algorithm	Cryptographic hash function that returns a string of fixed length
K	Know-Your-Customer (KYC)	The process of requiring users to perform an identity verification
L	Ledger	A record of financial transactions
M	Mint	The process of issuing new coins or tokens

212

Index	Term	Description
O	Oracle	Services which provide real-world data onto blockchains and smart contracts
	Orderbook	An electronic list of buy and sell orders
P	Peer-to-Peer (P2P)	A network where each node has equal permission to validate data. It allows two individuals to interact directly with each other without the need for a third party
	Private Key	Secret key that allows the user to spend cryptocurrencies in the wallet
	Protocol	A set of rules and procedures for transmitting data between computers
	Proof-of-Work (PoW)	A consensus algorithm in which a block is validated via work done in the form of mathematical hashing
S	Seed phrases	A group of words that allow access to cryptocurrency wallets
	Smart Contracts	Digital contracts that are powered by code
T	Two-factor authentication	An additional layer of security added to the authentication process
	Tokens	A unit of digital asset, usually coins issued on existing blockchains
W	Wallet	An interface that is used for cryptocurrencies storage. It is usually the interaction bridge between a user and the blockchain.

www.ingramcontent.com/pod-product-compliance
Lightning Source LLC
Chambersburg PA
CBHW070535220526
45467CB00003B/956